Anne Marshall

John and Mimi

May 1960

THE TRAGEDY OF NAN
AND OTHER PLAYS

THE
TRAGEDY OF NAN
and other plays by
John Masefield

New York & London
MITCHELL KENNERLEY
1912

Copyright 1909
By JOHN MASEFIELD

CONTENTS

THE TRAGEDY OF NAN

ACT I

SCENE:— *A kitchen in the house of a small tenant farmer at Broad Oak, on Severn.* 1810.
(*MRS PARGETTER and JENNY rolling dough and cutting apples.*)
(*JENNY takes flour from cupboard.*)

JENNY. It do seem quiet 'ere, Mother, after service.

MRS. P. P'raps now I'll 'ave some quiet.

JENNY. Only think, Mother, the ladies 'ad cups of tea in bed of a morning.

MRS. P. P'raps now you're come 'ome, I'll 'ave my cup of tea, it's time I'd a little something after all I gone through.

JENNY. Why, Mother?

MRS. P. What with that girl—Mooning round with 'er great eyes.

JENNY. Do 'ee mean Cousin Nan, Mother?

MRS. P. Mind your work. I wish them groceries'd come.

JENNY. Us'll 'ardly 'ave the things ready, Mother. Company be coming at dark.

MRS. P. Things'll 'ave to be ready. 'Old your tongue.

JENNY. 'Oo be coming, Mother, besides Dick Gurvil?

7

MRS. P.   Young Artie Pearce, wold Gaffer Pearce, them girls o' Robertses, and Tommy Arker.

JENNY.   Us shall be quite a pearty, shan't us?

MRS. P.   It won't be much of a pearty to me, with that Nan in the room.   She tokens 'er dad too much.

JENNY.   Why, Mother?

MRS. P.   Always so prim and well be'aved, thinking 'erself so much better than anyone.

JENNY.   Ah!

MRS. P.   Always 'elping 'er friends as she calls them.

JENNY.   'Elpin' them, Mother?

MRS. P.   Barthin' their brats for 'em.   'Oo knows what dirt they've been playing in?   Or mending their linen.   Flying in the face of Providence.   She might bring us all the fever.   (*going over to get a chair*) 'Ow many more times am I to tell yer I won't 'ave your things left about?   Look 'ere at this chair.

JENNY.   What be it, Mother?

MRS. P.   Look 'ere at your coat.   'Oo's to get you a new coat when this is wore out?   I will 'ave you careful.   Every day of my life I'm putting your clothes away.   Idle lawkamercy girl—

JENNY.   That ben't mine, Mother. That be Cousin Nan's.

MRS. P.   It's a wonder you couldn't say so at once.   Oh! so it's 'ers, is it.   Wot's she got in 'er pockets, I wonder. (*looks in pockets*) Wot's 'ere.   Oh! ribbons for our white neck, indeed.   Wot's 'ere.   Ho, indeed. (*taking paper*)

JENNY.   Wot's that, Mother, a letter?

MRS. P.   So this is wot's up, is it? (*she glances at paper*)

JENNY.   (*peeping*) It looks like Dick Gurvil's 'and, Mother—

8

MRS. P. You 'eed your duty. (*puts paper in her own pocket*) I'll give it 'er. 'Ere, out of my way. None of your rags in my way. (*flinging coat into a corner*)

JENNY. Oh, Mother, it's gone into the pigwash.

MRS. P. Wot if it 'as?

JENNY. She won't be able to wear it again, Mother. Never.

MRS. P. Let 'er go cold. Learn 'er not to leave 'er things about. Where are you going now?

JENNY. I was just going to hang it out, Mother.

MRS. P. Don't you dare to touch it. Stand 'ere and do your work. Let that dirty gallus bird do 'er own chores.

JENNY. Whatever do 'ee mean, Mother?

MRS. P. A gallus bird; that's all she is.

JENNY. Cousin Nan, Mother. Why do 'ee call 'er that?

MRS. P. Oh, p'raps your Father 'aven't a-told you.

JENNY. No, Mother.

MRS. P. Run and see if that be Dick with the groceries.

JENNY. (*goes to window*) No, Mother.

MRS. P. Drat 'im. Well, this mustn't go beyond yer—it ain't to be known about. 'Er father— your cousin Nan's father—wot married your father's sister—

JENNY. Yes, Mother.

MRS. P. Don't interrup' when your Mother's talking to yer. 'Er father, as she's so stuck on— 'E was 'ung.

JENNY. 'Ung, Mother?

MRS. P. At Glorster ja-il.

JENNY. Whatever 'ad 'e gone for to do?

MRS. P. 'E stole a sheep. That's wot 'e did.

9

JENNY. And so 'e were 'ung.

MRS. P. There's a thing to 'appen in a family.

JENNY. So be that why Nan come 'ere?

MRS. P. Thanks to your father.

JENNY. I didn't think, when I left service I should 'sociate with no gallus birds.

MRS. P. Nor you wouldn't if your father was in 'is right mind. The Lord 'ath laid a 'eavy judgmink on your father. Wot 'e wants with 'er I can't think.

JENNY. Her may remind he of Auntie.

MRS. P. 'E's no call to be reminded of any woman, 'cept 'er the Lord 'ath bound to 'im. Wot I gorn through with that Nan in the 'ouse'd a kill a Zebedee. They do say they be 'ard to kill.

JENNY. 'Ere be Father coming.

MRS. P. 'E 'as 'is lunch of a mornin' now. Take 'is cider off the 'ob.

JENNY. Where's 'is bread and cheese? (*she takes mug off hob, looks about carelessly, and drops and smashes mug on hearth*)

MRS. P. There now.

JENNY. Oh, Mother, I've broke it.

MRS. P. What a clumsy 'and you 'ave.

JENNY. It's Father's fav'rit mug. O Mother, whatever will 'e say.

MRS. P. 'Ere. Get upstairs. Get into the next room.

JENNY. Whatever will 'e say! 'E will be mad. (*cries*)

MRS. P. I'll talk 'im round. There! It's all a accident. Quick! before 'e comes now.

JENNY. 'E will be that mad! A dear, a dear! (*goes out*)

MRS. P. (*taking out letter*) So this is wot it's come to: (*declaiming*) Dick Gurvil to 'is fond beloved:

10

"As I was a-walking a lady I did meet
I knew it for my true love by the roses on 'er
    cheek
The roses on 'er cheek so sweetly did grow
    My 'eart out of my bosom, like a engine did go."
I'll watch yer Master Dick.

(*ENTER MR. PARGETTER, walking with a
stick. He is an old, shortish thick-set man, still hale*)

MR. P. (*advancing towards MRS. P. and gravely
saluting*) Well, Mother.

MRS. P. Did you see the fiddler?

MR. P. I saw the fiddler.

MRS. P. Is 'e coming to-night?

MR. P. 'E is coming. Us be going to 'ave great
wonders to-night. 'Ot mutton parsty pies.

MRS. P. You won't eat of no 'ot mutton parsty
pies. You know 'ow that sheep died as well as I do.
'E was *oovy*. (*pause*) A apple parsty's no great
wonders.

MR. P. A fiddler *and* a apple parsty's wonders.

MRS. P. It'll fare to be a girt wonder if th' apple
parsty be set. The amount of 'elp I get in the 'ouse-
work—

MR. P. At it again.

MRS. P. Yes, I am at it again, as you call it.

MR. P. What is it, now?

MRS. P. 'Ow much longer 'ave I got to put up
with that Nan in the 'ouse?

MR. P. My niece Nan'll stay in this 'ouse till—
till I go to churchyard. Or—till she marries. (*a
pause*) Now you know my mind. The girl's a
good girl, if you'd let up in your naggin' 'er 'ed off.

MRS. P. Naggin', Will?

MR. P. 'Ow's any girl to be good with you naggin' 'er 'ed off all day long.

MRS. P. When did I ever nag, as you call it?

11

MR. P. When? 'Ave you ever give 'er a kind word since she come 'ere.

MRS. P. I 'ave my 'eavenly warrant for all I done, Will. Them as the Lord afflicts we must come out from and be ye separate.

MR. P. I wonder the Lord can let you prosper, talking like that.

MRS. P. 'E knows 'is own, Will. You mark my words.

MR. P. I will mark 'em. And you mark mine. You'll treat my niece Nan as you'd treat your daughter Jenny.

MRS. P. Our daughter Jenny is the child of respectable parents. That—that charity girl is the daughter of—

MR. P. My sister. That's 'oo she's the daughter of.

MRS. P. And a thief 'oo was 'ung. I've always been respectable; and I've always kep' my girl respectable. I will not 'ave to do with the common and the unclean.

MR. P. You'll 'ave Nan 'ere, and you'll stop your nagging jealous tongue.

MRS. P. Jealous?

MR. P. Yes, jealous. You make 'er life a burden acos she tokens my sister. You was sweet on 'er dad yourself. That's why you make 'er life a burden.

MRS. P. Ho, indeed! Ha, ha, ha! Wot notions.

MR. P. That's the truth though. I know yer. I seen somethink of yer in these twenty years.

MRS. P. 'Ark you to me, Will Pargetter. Could you look on and see your daughter wronged?

MR. P. What's that got to do with it.

MRS. P. I'll tell you. When first we 'ad that charity girl 'ere—

12

MR. P. You call 'er Nan. Wot are you waivin' that bit of paper at me for?

MRS. P. We 'ad 'opes as our Jenny'd marry Dick Gurvil soon as she come back from service.

MR. P. That depended on Dick, not on Jenny.

MRS. P. Oh, but Dick was no difficulty. They kep' company before Jenny went to service. Dick was sweet on 'er all right.

MR. P. Dick was sweet on twenty girls.

MRS. P. No. Since that—that idle mooner come 'ere—Dick's been sweet on 'er. Look 'ere. Look at this. (*shews letter*)

MR. P. I don't want no letter. Put it where yer got it. That's the best thing I ever 'eard of Dick. Dick wants a wife with sense.

MRS. P. You'll let 'er marry 'im, after 'is carrying on along o' Jenny. And break your own daughter's 'art.

MR. P. Jenny's got no 'art.

MRS. P. Jenny'd resolve 'er 'eavenly crown for Dick Gurvil. 'Ow dare you blacken your own child?

MR. P. Blacken 'er. She's a cold 'eartless little baggage, Jenny is. Our Nan's worth a 'undred of 'er.

MRS. P. And you expect me to see that great-eyed, ugly, scrawf marrying my daughter's man.

MR. P. He's not your daughter's man. Dick's everybody's daughter's man. If 'e steps up and marries our Nan—it'll be the making of 'im. Give me my lunch.

MRS. P. Ah! I was forgetting. You put me out of patience. I'm afraid I spoke 'asty, Will. I've a 'asty tongue (*with suavity*)

MR. P. There, there! Where's my vittles? (*She puts down bread and cheese*)

1.3

(*PARGETTER gets up to fetch mug from the hob*)

MR. P. Thank ye, Mother. (*he sees the mug broken*) Law, Mother. You 'aven't a broke my Toby.

MRS. P. There, there now, Will, it was a accidenk.

MR. P. Not my Toby, broken?

MRS. P. It was a accidenk. (*she picks up the pieces*)

MR. P. 'Ooever 'ave a broke my Toby. Why weren't I told to onst?

MRS. P. She were goin' to tell yer, she said.

MR. P. Not—not Nan? It wasn't Nan broke it?

MRS. P. 'Er said 'er'd tell you to onst. It was a accidenk.

MR. P. But no accidenk could a broke my Toby.

MRS. P. There, there. Us'll buy another's good as 'er.

MR. P. But I've a 'ad my zider outen ov 'er this fifty year, like my gran'fer 'ave a-done. I'd a value for that Toby.

MRS. P. 'Er'll tell 'ee 'ow it was. It was a accidenk. She was in a 'urry, you see. Getting things ready for the pearty. It was quite a accidenk.

MR. P. 'Ow could it be quite a accidenk?

MRS. P. 'Er 'ands were wet, you see; she's particular about 'er 'ands—

MR. P. Clumsy 'anded—

MRS. P. They was all soapy from washing. It was quite a accidenk.

MR. P. And so she let it slip.

MRS. P. She didn't see where she was going. The sun was in 'er eyes or somethink. She's goin' to tell yer 'ow it was.

MR. P. My wold Toby jug as Granfer 'ad. 'Er could a broak my 'eart sooner. 'Er could. 'Er

14

could. (*he pushes away his bread and cheese*) I can't eat my vittles after that. That I can't. Careless girt gowk!

(*ENTER NAN—OLD PARGETTER stares at her hard all through this scene*)

NAN. You be back early, Uncle.

MRS. P. Well?

NAN. Yes, Aunt.

MRS. P. "Yes, aunt". 'Ave you looked at yourself long enough in the glass?

NAN. What glass?

MRS. P. The glass upstairs.

NAN. The beds are made. I suppose that's what you mean.

MRS. P. That's not the way to talk before your uncle.

NAN. May I help you cut them apples, Aunt?

MRS. P. No, you mayn't 'elp me cut these apples. You get your own work.

NAN. I've done all my work, Aunt.

MRS. P. None of your impudence. (*very sharply*)

NAN. I have.

MRS. P. If you 'ave, it's not done properly I know. I've a good mind to make you do it over. A very good mind.

NAN. Is that the dough for the pasty?

MRS. P. None o' yer business.

(*NAN picks up a rolling pin*)

Put down that pin when you're told.

NAN. I wish you'd let me 'elp, Aunt? Comp'ny be coming at dark.

MRS. P. What's it to do with you? I know w'en comp'ny's coming without your dinnin' it into me.

(*NAN goes softly to the dresser*)

Wot are you creepin' about on tiptoe for? One'd think you were a thief, like your father.

15

NAN. (*meekly*) I didn't want to disturve you, Aunt.

MRS. P. Disturve me! You couldn't disturve me more if you tried.

NAN. I'm sorry, Aunt.

MRS. P. You know that perfectly well.

NAN. I'm sorry, Aunt.

MRS. P. 'Ere, you give me the fidgets.

NAN. 'Ave you one of your sick headaches, Aunt?

MRS. P. You give me the sick'edache. One would think you might 'ave 'ad a little gratitood.

NAN. When I *was* grateful you called me a 'ipocrit.

MRS. P. Oh! *When* was you grateful, as you call it?

NAN. When I first come 'ere. I did my best, I did. I thought you'd like me if I work' 'ard, and 'elped you.

MRS. P. Did yer think!

NAN. I used to make you tea afore you got up of a morning: I wash up the dinner things, so as you could 'ave your nap of a afternoon. I never let you do the week's washing, not once, since I come 'ere.

MRS. P. One 'ud expect a little something. After all that's been done for you.

NAN. Done for me! What have you ever done for me?

MRS. P. Given you a 'ome.

NAN. A home?

MRS. P. There's not many would 'ave took in a girl 'er dad being 'ung. But I says to your Uncle—

NAN. I know what you said to Uncle. That the Rector 'ad asked you to take me in. That's what you said to Uncle. You was afeared the Rector'd let it be known if you refused. You was afeared folk'd get to know you for what you are. That's

16

why you took me in. (*more softly*) D'ye think I don't know, Aunt. I feel I do. (*pause*) And down in the shop they tell me what a friend you've been to me. "Mrs. Pargetter 'ave been kind tiv ee'', they say. And Mrs. Drew at the Rectory. She's another. "'Ow grateful you must feel towards your aunt." That's what she says. And you smile. You take it all in smiling. You lick your lips over all their praise. Or you play the martyr. You play the martyr. D'ye think I haven't heard you? "A lot of return I get," that's what you say. They praise you for being good to me. *Good! You!* And you make my life here a hell. You lick your lips to make life hell to me. And you tell lies about me. You mean woman. You so holy, you tell lies.

MR. P. (*angrily*) Now none of that now. That's enough. You leave the room.

MRS. P. No, she'll not leave the room. I'll learn 'er to be'ave first. (*to NAN*) I'd 'ave you remember as your daily bread as you're so fond of is give you by me and your Uncle.

NAN. Given me?

MRS. P. Per'aps you'll deny as you 'ave your food—God knows you eat enough.

NAN. And every morsel bitter. Bitter. You make it burn in my throat.

MRS. P. And a roof over your 'ed, which is more than your merits.

NAN. So 'as a man in a prison a roof.

MRS. P. Yes. You're right. 'E 'as till 'e's 'ung. And you 'ave your clothes. The very clothes on your back. Talking of clothes, that reminds me. Take that dirty coat of yours out of the pig wash where you put it. I suppose you want to poison the pigs next.

17

NAN. (*turning to pig wash trow*) Oh! 'Oo've bin and done that? (*at the point of tears*) I suppose you think it funny to spoil a poor girl's clothes. And now it's spoiled. (*she takes ribbon from pocket*) And this is spoiled. What I'd saved up for. Now I shan't have any. You put that in the trow. You know you did.

MRS. P. You say I put your dirty things in the trow and I'll put you in. Talk like that to me, will yer? One of these days I'll give you the cart whip, like what you deserve.

NAN (*turning to hide tears*). You read your Bible, and you go to church, and you do a thing like that. You put a poor girl's coat in the trow and as good as deny it afterwards.

MR. P. Now come, come, come. 'Ow d'yer expect to be ready for to-night? Let's ave no more catanddoggin' here.

MRS. P. I'm not talking to you. 'Old yer peace. (*furiously at interruption*) I'm talking to *you* (*To NAN*) You're a black, proud, ungrateful cat. Wot your 'eart'll look like on the Day of Judgemink beats me.

NAN. Oh! (*contemptuously—she opens out the sopping coat*)

MRS. P. I'll give yer 'oh'. 'Ere. Don't go dripping the pig wash all about the place. You drop it. Give it to me 'ere—'ere. (*she snatches at the coat and tries to wrench it from NAN's hands*)

NAN. Don't you dare to touch it. Let go of it.

MRS. P. Will yer. Leggo now.

NAN. I won't. No you don't. You'll tear it in another minute. I'll kill you if you tear it.

MRS. P. Wot'll you?

NAN. I'll kill you. I'll kill you.

MRS. P. (*putting both hands to the coat and wrench-*

18

ing it free; then slashing it into NAN's face) I'll
show you 'oo's mistress 'ere, my lady. Now—see.
(*she tears the collar off and stamps on it*) There.
You'll do what you're told 'ere, my lady.

(*NAN holds table and glares at her aunt then
picks up the cutting knife*)

NAN. (*slowly*) My dad gave me that coat. (*a
pause*) My dad.

MRS. P. Mind, Will, she's got the knife in 'er 'and.

PAR. (*going to her*) Give me thicky knife. (*he
takes it from her*) No temper 'ere. I've got one
score against you already. Wot's come to you to-
day?

MRS. P. The devil's come to 'er. She's pretty
near tore my arm off.

NAN. (*slowly*) You be careful.

MRS. P. But I'll teach yer.

NAN. You be careful.

PAR. Nan, you go to your room.

(*NAN sullenly picks up the torn coat and then
bursts into tears*)

NAN. My dad give me this coat. It's a dear coat.
(*she smooths out the torn and crumpled stuff*) And
now it's all torn. (*The PARGETTERS watch her with
a sort of hard scorn*) I'll never be able to wear en
again. Oh, my dad, I wish I was dead. I wish I
was dead.

PAR. No sinful talk like that, now. I won't 'ave it.

NAN. Uncle! I 'ave tried, I 'ave, Uncle.

PAR. Don't turn to me, girl. You'd ought to turn
to God—giving way to the devil—No—and you've
not been straight. If you'd told me at once I'd
'ave let it pass. Though I felt it. (*a pause, then
testily*) Come now, be straight. That's above all
things.

(*a pause, NAN sobs*)

19

Eh?

(*NAN sobs*)

MR. P. (*rising*) 'Aven't you something to tell me?

NAN. No! No!

PAR. (*grimly*) I thought you 'ad. (*turning*)

NAN. Oh, Uncle! Do 'ee.

MR. P. (*going*) I didn't think it of you.

NAN. Uncle.

MR. P. I didn't think it.

(*EXIT*)

MRS. P. (*going up to her*) I'll make your belly bitter, like in the Bible.

NAN. You! Oh! (*turns from her*) Oh, Dad, I wish I were with 'ee, I do.

MRS. P. (*bitterly*) You'll spoil yer looks for to-night, I shouldn't wonder. You won't ave yer young men neighing after yer. Dirty 'ogs.

(*NAN picks up apples and begins to cut them, still crying*)

MRS. P. I'll watch you with your young men! I'm not going to 'ave no mothers coming round complaining.

NAN. (*slowly*) I 'ope you may never feel wot I feel.

(*ENTER JENNY*)

JENNY. Mawther!

MRS. P. 'Ush!

JENNY. There be Dick's trap with the groceries.

MRS. P. Time too. 'Ere (*to NAN*) go and get them!

NAN. Me?

MRS. P. Yes, you. 'Oo else. Do something for your living for once in a way.

(*EXIT NAN*)

JENNY. Mother, wot 'ave Dad say?

20

MRS. P. 'Ush yer tongue. I've made *that* right.

JENNY. O mother. I thort 'e'd 'ave my 'ed off for it.

MRS. P. Never you 'eed of that. I've somethink else to say to you. That girl, Nan—

JENNY. Wot, Mother?

MRS. P. (*speaking very rapidly*) You better watch out she don't tread a thy corns, as well as thy mother's she've a done.

JENNY. Wot do 'ee mean, mother?

MRS. P. Dick Gurvil's 'oo I mean.

JENNY Oh!

MRS. P. Yes, Dick Gurvil! She've set 'er cap at Dick.

JENNY. Oh!

MRS. P. (*mimicking*) Oh! Oh! *Yes*, and Dick be sweet on 'er.

JENNY. I don't care, mother.

MRS. P. Yes, you do care. 'Ave done o' your folly.

JENNY. Dick can please 'isself so far as I'm concerned, I'm sure.

MRS. P. No 'e can't please 'isself, as you call it. 'Oo else'd yer get if you lose 'im? You take a man when you can get 'im. There ain't too many, let me tell yer.

JENNY. I do-an't care, I'm sure. I don't want no men.

˙ MRS. P. Don't you want. You listen to me. You got ter want. Whether you like or not. I ain't goin' to 'ave you the talk of the town.

JENNY. Lor, mother! I didn't think of that.

MRS. P. No, I know you didn't think.

JENNY. Lor, mother.

MRS. P. 'Oo 'ad 'er man took by a gallus-bird.

JENNY˙ Would they say that, Mother?

21

MRS. P. 'Oo's she to take Dick Gurvi'? If you'd any pride—

JENNY. Be you sure she be a-trying for Dick?

MRS. P. Well, you best find out.

JENNY. I'll watch it, I will.

MRS. P. (*as NAN ENTERS*) Ah! you'd a better! Now I got to see to the 'ouse work. I'll expect you to 'ave everythink ready against I come back. (*to NAN*) You may think as you're someone. I'll learn you different. None o' your tricks, 'ere. No! Nor none of your mother's carryings on (*a pause*) with men. That's wot I mean . . . . Gallus bird.

(*She goes out, NAN draws a chair to the table— JENNY is already seated—and begins to cut apples. She is crying. She gathers the torn coat together tenderly*)

JENNY. Never mind Mother, Nan. She don't mean nothin!

NAN. I don't—

JENNY. She be only put out by 'avin' comp'ny to-night.

NAN. It's not! It's not! Oh, she'd ought to leave my father.

JENNY. There, there now—let I get 'ee some warm warter off the 'ob. Your eyes'll be as red as red.

NAN. I don't care, I don't care.

JENNY. Why, come now. Us be going to be girt friends, us be, ben't us? Mother be a 'ard woman to please. But 'er don't mean it.

NAN. Her do speak so bitter. They be all against me! The 'ole world be against me.

JENNY. (*with bowl of water and a handkerchief*) Do 'ee jest mop thy eyes. Or let I.

NAN. It be kind of you to trouble. What a girt silly I be to cry so!

22

JENNY. Your eyes'll be as red. Come, come! There be 'andsome young men a-comin'. I wouldn't wonder as they be all sweet on you! I wouldn't wonder as you'd 'ave a sweet'eart some Easter.

NAN. A sweet'eart! A charity girl!

JENNY. Don't take it to 'eart. Us be goin' to be friends, ben't us, dear?

NAN. It be kind of you to speak kind.

JENNY. And us'll go out of a Sunday. Why, us'll be girt friends. It go to my 'eart to think of thy trouble.

NAN. Will 'ee be a friend, cousin Jenny?

JENNY. There, there. Wot pretty eyes you 'ave. Your 'air's thicker than mine. 'Ow you do a set it off. Us'll 'ave no secrets, will us?

NAN. 'Ee will be my friend, won't 'ee, Jenny? Do-an't 'ee be agen me—I couldn't bear it if you turned against me. I've sometimes been near killing myself since I came here. Your Mother's been that bitter to me.

JENNY. Don't 'ee say such things.

NAN. Jenny, I'll tell 'ee why I didn't kill myself.

JENNY. Lord, Nan, doa-n't 'ee.

NAN. I want 'ee to bear with me, Jenny. I'll tell 'ee why I didn't kill myself. I thought . . . . there . . . . it's only nonsense. Did you ever think about men, Jenny? About loving a man? About marriage?

JENNY. I've 'oped to 'ave a 'ome of my own. And not to be a burden 'ere and that.

NAN. Ah! But about 'elping a man?

JENNY. A man 'as strength. 'E ought to 'elp a woman.

NAN. I could 'elp a man, Jenny.

JENNY. Wot ideyers you do 'ave!

23

NAN. When a girl's 'eart is breaking, Jenny, she 'as ideyers.

JENNY. Ah!

NAN. Jenny!

JENNY. Yes, Nan?

NAN. I've never talked to a woman like this afore. I felt I'd die if I couldn't talk to someone.

JENNY. I know, exackly!

NAN. When I see you so kind, and you so pretty Jenny, I felt I must speak.

JENNY. Do you think me pretty, Nan?

NAN. Yes, Jenny.

JENNY. In service they thought me pretty. All but cook.

NAN. You are pretty, Jenny.

JENNY. Cook was a unpleasant old thing. She did 'er 'air in papers. No ladies do their 'air in papers! Ow! she was 'orrid of a morning. O! the waste I see go on in that 'ouse. They 'ad pastry every day. And the ladies had milk and biscuits at eleven of a morning.

NAN. You must tell me all your secrets, Jenny.

JENNY. That I will. And will 'ee tell I all yourn?

NAN. If you like, Jenny.

JENNY. And will 'ee tell I when you 'ave a sweet-'eart?

NAN. Ah! A sweet'eart. You must tell me about yours, Jenny.

JENNY. Ah! I ain't got one yet.

NAN. 'Aven't you, Jenny?

JENNY. Noa. Not one special like.

NAN. You'll 'ave one soon, Jenny. O Jenny, I hope you'll be very 'appy.

JENNY. Love be queer, ben't it? The things it makes people do. Could 'ee fancy a man, Nan?

NAN. Perhaps.

24

JENNY. Ugly girt scrawfs, I think they be.

NAN. Not all of them.

JENNY. Perhaps you 'ave a fancy, Nan? 'Ave you, dear. 'Ave you? 'Oo be it, Nan? Tell me, dearie. I wouldn't tell a single soul. Tell me, Nan. You said as you'd 'ave no secrets from me.

NAN. Ah!

JENNY. Is it anyone I know?

(*NAN goes to her and puts an arm round her and kisses her*)

NAN. Yes, dear.

JENNY. Be it Artie Pearce?

NAN. No, Jenny.

JENNY. 'Oo be it. It be a shame not to tell me!

NAN. Jenny dear?

JENNY. Yes, Nan. Tell me now. Whisper.

NAN. It be Dick Gurvil, Jenny.

JENNY. Dick Gurvil?

NAN. I love him. I love him.

JENNY. Do you love him very much?

NAN. It feel like my 'eart was in flower, Jenny.

JENNY. Ah! It must. (*a pause*) I 'ope you'll be very 'appy. You and Mr. Gurvil.

NAN. God bless you, Jenny.

JENNY. What eyes you have got, cousin Nan. To think of you fancying Dick! It *be* nice to 'ave you for a friend, cousin Nan.

NAN. Kiss me, dear. You've never kissed me.

JENNY. There! Go and bathe thy eyes, Nan. They'll be red if 'ee don't. 'Ee mustn't 'ave them red for Dick to-night. Bathe 'em in cold.

NAN. I could cry, I could. (*she goes slowly out*)

JENNY. (*at the other door*) Mother. (*a pause*) (*softly*) Mother.

MRS. P. (*off*) Yes!

JENNY. Come 'ere a moment

25

MRS. P. (*wiping her hands*) What d'yer want now.

JENNY. About Nan.

MRS. P. Wot? Wot about 'er?

JENNY. (*giggling*) She be soft on Dick, Mother. Her've a-told me.

MRS. P. Ho!

JENNY. (*giggling*) Us'll 'ave to watch it, Mother.

MRS. P. I'll watch it.

CURTAIN

ACT II

SCENE:—The kitchen. NAN tidying up. She places tray, glasses and bottle in inner room

NAN.   (*sings*) . . . .

> Blow, blow, thou winds of winter blow,
> And cover me with sparklen snow,
> And tear the branches from the tree,
> And strew the dead leaves over me.

DICK.   (*coming in*) Miss Nan.

NAN.   Why, Mr. Gurvil! What a start you give me. You be early.

DICK.   Ah? When'll the others be 'ere?

NAN.   Not yet. It's not half past yet.

DICK.   When'll the others—Mrs. Pargetter—be down?

NAN.   They won't be down this ten minutes. They be dressing.

DICK.   And 'aven't the fiddler come?

NAN.   No.

DICK.   Per'aps I'd a better go out again.

NAN.   No. Come in and sit down, Mr. Dick. They'll be 'ere direckly. I'll be gone. Tell me the news in the great world. What be 'appening?

DICK.   They do say there be a criminal a-broak loose. Out of Glorster jail.

NAN.   Indeed!

DICK.   And come 'idin' 'ere somewhere, they think.

NAN. What makes them think that?

DICK. I dunno. But there be a Bow Street Runner. And there be a gentleman come. They were askin' where Parson live. They must be 'avin' a hue and cry. Hope they'll catch 'im and 'ang 'im. I'd like to sick the dogs at 'em.

NAN. They be 'uman beings, like us be, Mr. Dick.

DICK. (*undoing his neck-cloth*) No, they ben't like us. That be where you women go wrong. Along of your 'earts, that is. I'd like to see all criminals 'anged. Then us honest ones might fare to prosper. (*He takes off neck-cloth*)

NAN. What'll you take, Mr. Dick, after your walk?

DICK. What be going?

NAN. 'Ave some zider and a cake. They be in the next room, ready.

DICK. If it ben't troubling you, I ull.

(*NAN fetches mug and plate*)

DICK. (*taking a cake*) I'd ought to be a-waiting on you, not you a-waiting on me. Only I 'avent any angel-cakes 'ere. None but angel-cakes 'd be fit eating for you, Miss Nan.

NAN. Oh, now, I wonder how many girls you've made that speech to.

DICK. None, I never.

NAN. Well, I hope you like your cake?

DICK. It be beautiful. A spice-cake, when it be split and buttered, and just set to the fire, so as the butter runs. I don't mean to toast it; but just set to the fire, and then just a sprinkle of sugar to give it a taste. No so as to make it sweet, you know. It go down like roses. Like kissing a zweet 'eart at 'arvest time. When the girt moon be zhining.

NAN. If they be all that to you, Mr. Dick, you

28

must 'ave another. Try and think the clock be the
moon a-zhining.

(*she gets more cakes*)

DICK. It be lovely 'aving cakes and you bringing
them to me. (*Bites*) But there ben't no sugar, not
on this one. Miss Nan, will 'ee jest put thy pretty
'and on this cake, and then it'll be sugared lovely.

NAN. I'm not going to do anything so silly. 'Ere.
Take this one. This one be sugared.

DICK. (*eating*) It 'ud be just 'eaven if you'd
'ave 'alf of it. So's I might feel—some'ow—as—

NAN. No. I won't 'ave any. 'Ave another drop
of zider.

DICK. (*tasting*) Your zider be too peert, Miss
Nan. I like zider to be peert, like I likes my black
puddens done, up to a point. But zider's peert's
this—I tell you what it want. It want to 'ave a
apple roast therein, and a sod toast therein, and then
it want to 'ave a nutmeg grated ever so light, not
rough, yer know. And then it be made mellow,
like, like tart of a Sunday.

NAN. Why, Mr. Dick, you'd ought to have been
a cook, I think.

DICK. My father say to me—"Mind thy innards",
he say. I 'ad to do for my father, arter mother died.
Very pertiklar about his innards dad were. I learned
about innards from 'im.

NAN. It be wonderful to 'ave a father to do for.
To think as he knowed 'ee when you were a little
un. To think as perhaps 'e give up lots o' things,
so's you might fare to be great in the world.

DICK. My dad never give up. 'E said 'e try it
once, just to try like. It never'd 'ave suit my dad.

NAN. It be always 'ard for a man to give up, even
for a child, they say. But a woman 'as to give up.
You don't know. You never think per'aps what a

29

woman gives up. She gives up 'er beauty and 'er peace. She gives up 'er share of joy in the world. All to bear a little one; as per'aps'll not give 'er bread when 'er be wold.

DICK. I wonder women ever want to 'ave children. They be so beautiful avore they 'ave children. They 'ave their red cheeks, so soft. And sweet lips so red's red. And their eyes bright, like stars a-zhining. And oh, such white soft 'ands. Touch one of 'em, and you 'ave like shoots all down. Beau-ti-vul. Love-lee.

NAN. It be a proud thing to 'ave a beauty to raise love in a man.

DICK. And after. I seen the same girls, with their 'ands all rough of washing-day, and their fingers all scarred of stitching. And their cheeks all flaggin', and sunk. And dull as toads' bellies, the colour of 'em. And their eyes be 'eavy, like a foundered wold ewe's when 'er time be on 'er. And lips all bit. And there they do go with the backache on 'em. Pitiful, I call it. Draggin' their wold raggy skirts. And the baby crying. And little Dick with 'is nose all bloody, fallen in the grate. And little Sairey fell in the yard, and 'ad 'er 'air mucked. Ah! Ugh! It go to my 'eart.

NAN. Ah, but that ben't the all of love, Mr. Dick. It be 'ard to see beauty gone, and joy gone, and a light 'eart broke. But it be wonderful for to 'ave little ones. To 'ave brought life into the world. To 'ave 'ad them little live things knocking on your 'eart, all them months. And then to feed them. 'Elpless like that.

DICK. They be pretty, little ones be, when they be kept clean and that. I likes 'earing them sing 'imns. I likes watching the little boys zwimming in the river. They be so white and swift, washing

30

themselves. And the splashin' do shine zo. Dia-
monds. 'Oo be coming 'ere to-night—'sides us?

NAN. Old Gaffer Pearce be a-comin' to fiddle.

DICK. He'd ought to be in mad'ouse, Gaffer
did. Dotty owd gape. He ben't wholly stalwart in
uns brains, folk do observe. But—

NAN. He been a beautiful fiddler.

DICK. He been a wonder, that old man 'ave.

NAN. 'E play wonderful still, when 'e gets thinking of old times, and of 'is girl as 'e calls 'er. Why,
she've been dead fifty years and more.

DICK. She was beautiful. They call 'er the Star
of the West. My dad 'ave tell of 'er. She 'ad a
face like cream.

NAN. He made beautiful poems to 'er; and music,
'e did. I 'eard 'im sing 'is poems once. He was
fiddlin' quiet-like, all the time 'e were a-singing;
and the tears standing in 'is eyes. 'E's never been
quite right since the Lord 'ad mercy on 'er.

DICK. 'Oo else's comin' 'sides Gaffer?

NAN. Tommy and Artie. What a 'andsome boy
Artie be grown.

DICK. Ah? I 'ear 'em say that. I couldn't ever
see it.

NAN. He be just like his mother. Black and
comely.

DICK. I likes a good black. I likes a good brown,
a good bay brown. I likes a good black too. There
be bright blacks and there be dull blacks. Now
what be the black as I likes? Your 'air is jest the
very colour. Beautiful I call it.

NAN. (*getting up*) If you ben't going to 'ave
more zider I'll take your mug, Mr. Dick. Mr.
Dick.

DICK. Yes.

NAN. We've 'ad a sheep die on us last week,

Don't you 'ave none of our 'ot mutton pies to-night.

DICK. Ah? I 'ope you'll give me twice of trotters, instead like, I can do with a trotter, I can. I s'pose us be going to 'ave great times 'ere to-night, Miss Nan.

NAN. Yes, indeed. Us'll dance the moon down to-night.

DICK. I s'pose you be a girt lady to dance?

NAN. I've not dance now, for more'n a year, Mr. Dick.

DICK. I s'pose you 'ad dancings when you were to 'ome.

NAN. Us used to dance on our doorsteps at 'ome. There was an old man used to fiddle to us. Every night there was a moon, we danced. The girls would dance in their pattens. They used to go clack, clack, their feet did. You'd a thought it was drums, Mr. Dick.

DICK. I wish I'd bin there to 'ave dance with you.

NAN. And then we used to sing "Joan to the Maypole" and "Randal" and all the old songs. And there'd be beetles a buzzin'. And sometimes one of the shepherds come with 'is flute. It was nice at 'ome, then.

DICK. What times us be 'avin' since you come 'ere. It be always sad to leave 'ome. But I s'pose you'll be going back afore long. Your dad and your mother'll be a-wanting you. Sure to be.

NAN. They be dead, Mr. Dick.

DICK. Now, be they indeed! Mrs. Pargetter do talk's though you 'ad both your folk.

NAN. Mrs. Pargetter! She has 'er reasons, Mr. Dick, for letting folk think that.

DICK. What reasons can 'er 'ave for that, Miss Nan?

32

NAN. Some day, per'aps I'll tell you 'er reasons. Now let I take your coat and that.

(*She takes coat, hat, etc. and puts them in inner room. Then RE-ENTERS*)

DICK. 'Ow brave you be a-looking, Miss Nan.

NAN. Soap and water tells, they do say.

DICK. You be all roses, Miss Nan. And you be all lilies.

NAN. Why, Mr. Dick! You be quite the courtier.

DICK. Ah! (*producing a rose*) Miss Nan?

NAN. Yes?

DICK. I brought a rose—

NAN. For Jenny, Mr. Dick?

DICK. No, for 'ee. Will 'ee wear it, Miss Nan?

NAN. Yes, if you'll give it to me.

DICK. 'Ere it be. Will 'ee say thank you for it?

NAN. Thank you, Mr. Dick. What a beautiful rose!

DICK. 'Er be a Campden Wonder. 'Er be red. Like love. Love be red. Like roses.

NAN. Oh!

DICK. I see that rose growing, Miss Nan—an' I— I thought 'er'd look beautiful if—if—if you were wearing of 'er, like.

NAN. Well, I hope it does.

DICK. You put 'er to the blush, Miss Nan—Miss Nan—

NAN. Yes?

DICK. Will you do I a favour?

NAN. What is it?

DICK. Will 'ee wear that rose in your hair?

NAN. In my hair, Mr. Dick! Why?

DICK. I 'ad a dream once of you with roses in your hair.

NAN. (*putting rose in her hair*) In the old times women always put roses in their hair. When they

33

danced, they wore roses in their hair. The rose-leaves fell all about 'en, my mother told me.

DICK. It looks like it were growing out of your 'ed.

NAN. I must light the lamp.

DICK. No, don't 'ee. Don't 'ee.

NAN. (*striking a match*) They must have looked beautiful, those women must, in the old time. There was songs made of them. Beauty be a girt gift, Mr. Dick.

DICK. It be wonderful in a woman.

NAN. It makes a woman like God, Mr. Dick.

DICK. You be beautiful, Nan; you be beautiful.

NAN. Ah, Mr. Dick.

DICK. You be beautiful. You be like a fairy. The rose. You be beautiful like in my dream.

NAN. Ah! Let go my hands. Let go my hands.

DICK. You be beautiful. Your eyes. And your face so pale. And your hair with the rose. O Nan, you be lovely. You be lovely!

NAN. O don't! Don't!

DICK. My love, my beloved.

NAN. Ah!

DICK. I love you, O Nan, I love you.

NAN. Let me go: let me go, please.

DICK. Do 'ee care for me? Do 'ee love me, Nan?

NAN. You don't know! You don't know! You don't know about me.

DICK. I love you.

NAN. Ah! You mustn't. You mustn't love me.

DICK. There be no high queen 'as a beauty like yours, Nan.

NAN. O! let me go.

DICK. My love! My 'andsome!

NAN. O! Dick.

DICK. Nan, O Nan, do 'ee love me?

34

NAN. Ah!

DICK. Dear sweet. Will 'ee marry me? Do 'ee love me?

NAN. I love you, Dick.

DICK. My love! My pretty!

NAN. My dear love.

DICK. My beautiful. I'll make a song for you, my beautiful.

NAN. Your loving me, that's song enough.

DICK. Nan, dear, let I take the pins out of your hair. Let me 'ave your 'air all loose. Your lovely hair. O Nan, you be a beautiful woman.

NAN. Ah, God! I wish I were beautiful.

DICK. Dear love, you be.

NAN. More beautiful. Then I'd 'ave more to give you.

DICK. Kiss me. Kiss me!

NAN. There be my 'air, Dick. It ben't much, after all.

DICK. (*kissing the hair*) Oh, beautiful. Beau-ti-vul. My own Nan.

NAN. I am yours, my beloved.

DICK. When shall us be married? When shall us come together?

NAN. Ah, my love! Now is enough. Now is enough.

DICK. When shall us marry?

NAN. Kiss me.

DICK. Shall it be Michaelmas?

NAN. Kiss me. Kiss me.

DICK. My winsome. My beauty.

NAN. Now loose me, darling. (*They break*) I have had my moment. I have been happy.

DICK. Nan! Nan!

NAN. I cannot marry you. O Dick, 'ee must go away. Go away. (*He goes toward her*) Don't

35

'ee. Us can never marry. You'd 'ate me if you knew. I can't tell you. Not to-night, dear. They'll be coming down directly. If I married you, Dick? Oh, I can't. I can't—if I married you—if we lived 'ere—I might bring shame upon you. They'd call names after me. They'd know. They'd know.

DICK. My pretty! My Nan. Tell thy Dick.

NAN. Ah, no, no. Don't touch me. You don't know yet. I'm—not a fit—I'm not a fit woman for you to marry, Dick. My father. My poor dad— (*she breaks down*) O Dick! O Dick! You don't know what sorrows I gone through. I think my 'eart'll break.

DICK. There, there, Nan. Tell thy Dick. My poor dearie. You be my dear love now, Nan.

NAN. If you love me, Dick—O, my love! Us together! Us needn't fear what they say. Us could go away, Dick. To America. Us'd be 'appy there. O Dick, take me out of this. All we 'ave is our lives, Dick. With love, us'd never want. Us'd 'ave that, my love. Take me, Dick.

DICK. I'll take you, darling. To-night. To-night I'll tell them.

NAN. In spite of—even if—what I 'ave to say?

DICK. No matter what it is, dear. To-night, now. To-night. When the fiddler comes.

NAN. Ah! my beloved!

DICK. I'll claim you. Before them all, I'll claim you.

NAN. Your wife, my blessed.

DICK. Kiss me, once more, dear.

NAN. Before they come.

(*Outside the door there is a shuffling and giggling*)

A VOICE. They be in. I hear 'em.

A VOICE. They ben't.

A VOICE. Don't Artie. (*Together, rapidly*)

A VOICE. Sh!

A VOICE. All together.

A VOICE. One after the other.

DICK. Here they are.

NAN. My beloved! My own.

VOICES. "Joan, to the maypole away let us on
The time is short and will be gone—"

(*They stop and giggle*)

ANOTHER. They ben't.

(*One hums the tune*)

DICK. To-night. Before them all. When the fiddle begins. My wife.

NAN. My husband.

VOICES. "Where your beauties may be seen"
Bang! Bang! Bang!

(*They knock the door. The LOVERS break. Mrs. Pargetter and Jenny run downstairs as NAN flings the door open. ENTER OLD GAFFER PEARCE, ARTIE of that ilk, TOMMY ARKER and TWO GIRLS*)

MRS. P. 'Ere you be. 'Ow nice it is to see you. (*She kisses the girls and looks hard at NAN*)

JENNY. (*To DICK*) Ah, Mr. Gurvil. 'Ave you brought I the rose as you promised?

DICK. You don't want no roses.

JENNY. You ain't very polite, Mr. Dick.

DICK. You got roses in your cheeks, you 'ave.

MRS. P. 'Ow be you, gaffer?

(*General salutation*)

ARTIE. Granfer doan't 'ear you, unless you 'it 'im. (*shouts in his ear*) 'Ow be you, granfer?

GAFFER. (*looking at NAN*) Twice I seen her, twice. Her've gone by on the road. With a rose in 'er 'air. And 'er eyes shone. Twice. In April.

ARTIE. 'Ere, gaffer! Sit down 'ere. 'E can fiddle

37

still, th'owd granfer do; but 'e doan't talk, not to strangers.

A GIRL. Us seed some strangers in the village, Mrs. Pargetter.

MRS. P. Ah?

TOM. They were askin' where your 'ouse was. Them and parson.

ARTIE. 'Ave you been a-robbin', Mrs. Pargetter?

MRS. PAR. A-robbin'! No. I 'ave enough of thieves without me going stealin', I 'ope.

ARTIE. Well. One of 'em be a runner, 'e be.

DICK Yes, for I seed 'en too.

MRS. P. O! So you didn't come with th' others, then, Dick?

DICK. Noa. But I seen 'en.

ALL. I wonder whatever they do want!

MRS. PAR. Well. If they're coming 'ere, us shall soon know. I should a-thought the pleece could a-caught their own thieves.

(*OLD PARGETTER comes downstairs, buttoning his waistcoat*)

MR. P. Aha! Aha!

ALL. 'Ow be you, Mr. Pargetter?

MR. PAR. (*saluting*) Why, 'ow beautiful all you girls be looking! 'Ullo, Dick! You be quite the bridegroom. Why gaffer, what a old Pocahontas you be, to be sure! 'Ave you brought your fiddle?

GAFFER. (*still staring at NAN*) 'Oo be her? On the roads, shining, I've seen 'er. Scattering blossoms, blossoms.

JENNY. (*after glancing at GAFFER*) So you come 'ere early, Dick. Why Nan, do look. You 'aven't a-done your 'air. Look, mother, at Nan's 'air!

MRS. PAR. What in the name of Fate d'you 'ave that rose in your 'air for? Any why d'yer come down with your 'air like that?

NAN. I had to open the door. I had to light the candle.

GAFFER. Give I a cup of red wine and a cup of white wine, and honey (*coming towards her*) and a apple and a—I be goin' to fiddle joy to the feet of the bride.

ARTIE. You be going to do wonders, you be. Sit down, you old stupe. Ain't no bride 'ere.

MR. P. (*to the GIRLS*) There be brides for us all. With all you lovely young things. Nothing like 'aving a sweet'eart. Now! You ladies, you'll want to take off your things.

ARTIE. 'Ow about us?

MR. PAR. One sect at a time. Like the sheep goin' through a 'edge. Per'aps you ladies'll go upstairs with Nan and Jenny 'ere.

NAN. Come, Ellen.

JENNY. 'Ere! Give I your brolly.

(*The GIRLS go upstairs*)

MR. PAR. Now, you gentlemen. Come on in 'ere with me. (*He leads them to the inner room*)

MRS. PAR. (*as DICK follows*) Oh, Dick.

DICK. Ess, Mrs. Pargetter.

MRS. PAR. I see you 'ave your things off. Just 'elp me a moment, there's a good lad.

DICK. Ess, Mrs. Pargetter. What do 'e want done?

MRS. PAR. Us must 'ave all clear for dancing. I'll nip them candles over 'ere to the dresser. There. Now 'elp me lift the table over. There! You was 'ere early, wasn't yer, Dick?

DICK. Nothin' to speak of. 'Ow about them chairs?

MRS. PAR. They'll do nicely. I suppose Nan let you in?

DICK. Ess. Miss Nan done.

39

MRS. PAR. You two been 'aving a fine game, I know.

DICK. Ah?

MRS. PAR. Don't tell me you 'aven't. Did she kiss yer?

DICK. (*sullenly*) Never you mind.

MRS. PAR. Oh, I don't mind. But I got eyes, I 'ave.

DICK. Oh! What good 'ave they done yer?

MRS. PAR. O, when I see a girl with 'er face all flushed, and 'er 'air all 'anging down, and a rose stuck over 'er ear, and a young man by 'er as flustered as what you are—Well—I can—

DICK. What can you?

MRS. PAR. Well, I know they don't come like that of their own.

DICK. (*sullenly*) Do you?

MRS. PAR. I ain't blaming yer, mind.

DICK. Aren't yer?

MRS. PAR. I know what it is to be young, myself. But all the same—

DICK. What?

MRS. PAR. Oh, nothing.

DICK. What were you going to say?

MRS. PAR. Nothing.

DICK. You were going to say something.

MRS. PAR. No, I weren't. Only it mid seem strange. You see, your dad's so partikler.

DICK. Oh! 'Im.

MRS. PAR. 'As 'e took you in 'is partner yet? Your dad?

DICK. No.

MRS. PAR. No, I know 'e 'aven't. I could tell yer something. A little surprise—about your dad.

DICK. What's that?

MRS. PAR. Somethin' 'e said to me. I don't know as I've a right to tell yer.

40

DICK. About my being took in as partner to 'im?

MRS. PAR. It was meant as a secret. But there —since—us can 'ave no secrets, can us?

DICK. Why, no—I'm—

MRS. PAR. Well—your dad says to me, "Mrs. Pargetter" 'e says, "I'm gettin' to be a old man, I want to see my boy settled. Now then", 'e says. "The day my boy marries I 'ave 'im bound my part-ner. And £20 to 'elp 'im furnish".

DICK. Good iron! A old chanti-cleer. Balm in Gilead, as the saying is.

MRS. PAR. "Yes", I says, "And more no mother could ask". (*change of voice*) That girl'd forsake 'er 'eavenly crown for you, Dick. She's drooped like a lily of the vale since she's been away. If you'd seen that girl as I seen 'er, you'd 'ave yourself arst this Sunday. Or you'll 'ave 'er goin' into a decline. 'Ave you arst 'er yet?

DICK. Yes. I arst 'er just now. Just this minute ago.

MRS. PAR. When she was at the door 'ere?

DICK. When I come in.

MRS. PAR. Wot did she say, I wonder? No tellin', I suppose?

DICK. I thought as you'd seen. I mean, from what you said.

MRS. PAR. No. I never seed.

DICK. From 'er 'avin' 'er 'air down. The rose and that.

MRS. PAR. 'Air down? She 'adn't 'er 'air down. I done it myself.

DICK. Yes, she 'ad 'er 'air down. You said— just now—

MRS. PAR. Jenny 'ad?

DICK. No, Nan.

MRS. PAR. Nan: wot's she got to do with it?

41

DICK. I've just arst 'er to marry me, Mrs. Par-getter. And her 'ave said yes. (*a pause*) It'll be nice bein' a partner and that, won't it. I'll be able to 'ave the trap of a evenin'. And I'll 'ave money for—

MRS. PAR. (*grimly*) *You* be 'is partner! You'll be your dad's partner if you marry Jenny—that's your dad's arrangement. That's wot 'e's planned.

DICK My dad 'ave planned—

MRS. PAR. "'E shall marry as I choose", 'e says, "my son shall. If 'e don't know which side 'is bread is buttered, there's the door. 'E can beg."

DICK. 'E can beg!

MRS. PAR. "Not a penny will 'e ever 'ave from *me*", 'e says. Now.

DICK. So!

(*MRS. PARGETTER watches him*)

MRS. PAR. D'you think we'd let you throw Jen-ny over, after getting 'er talked about?

DICK. It be different 'avin' a kiss or two of a girl and wantin' to marry 'er.

(*RE-ENTER PARGETTER slowly, looking hard at DICK who is very white. He walks to the dresser, picks up a corkscrew, and walks slowly out, looking hard at DICK but saying nothing*)

MRS. PAR. Now then.

DICK. (*moistening his lips*) Per'aps my father'll 'ear me explain.

MRS. PAR. Wot'll you tell 'im?

DICK. Tell 'im as Jenny ain't no more to me 'n what a pig's milt is. Tell 'im as I love Nan. And as I be goin' to marry 'er.

MRS. PAR. (*slowly and grimly*) You'll tell 'im for instans, you'll tell your father, for instans, as you're goin' to marry a girl whose dad was 'ung at

42

Glorster, like the thief 'e was.   Just afore last Christmas.

DICK.   Nan's dad wos?

MRS. PAR.   (*nods her head*) And 'er mother 'ad
men come to see 'er. (*a pause*) 'Ow'll yer tell
that to yer dad?

DICK.   My Lord Almighty! Daughter of one of
them!

MRS. PAR.   Two of them.

DICK.   My 'oly Saviour!

MRS. PAR.   Your 'art out of your bosom like a
engine it does go.

DICK.   I'll marry 'er yet to spite yer.

MRS. PAR.   Wot'll yer marry 'er on? You ain't
got a penny. She ain't got a penny. (*a pause*) I
wonder she never told yer about 'er dad's being 'ung.
They 'ad yeomanry in front of the gaol. Quite an
affair. Didn't she never tell yer?

DICK.   No. 'Er was going to. My! Oh my——

MRS. PAR.   Per'aps she waited till she 'ooked yer.
'Ark at 'em in there!

(*Laughter inside and one crows like a cock*)

She is artful. I never see a deeper girl than wot
she is.

DICK.   Oh, 'old yer tongue, you old devil! I've
'ad my gruel.

MRS. PAR.   Come, come. Be a man.

DICK.   Mrs. Pargetter. I mean, I'm—Mrs. Pargetter—

MRS. PAR.   Yes? Wot?

DICK.   I dunno—I dunno wot to think.

MRS. PAR.   Your dad'll know wot to think.

DICK.   I dunno! If I 'ad a little of my own!

MRS. PAR.   Oh, if yer like to starve, starve. Walk.
Pad yer 'oof.

DICK.   Ah! A tramper! My 'eavenly King!

43

MRS. PAR. Lots on 'em pass 'ere. Dirt on 'em. Feet comin' through their boots. You see 'em nick crusts out of the gutter. Berries of a 'edge, some on 'em. Froze stiff, some on 'em, under a rick. Lots on 'em.

DICK. Ah! Don't! I can't! (*a pause*)

MRS. PAR. Well, Dick? Wot's it to be? Is it Jenny?

DICK. O damn it, yes, it's Jenny, Jenny. Like 'avin' a cold poultice! Very well, it's Jenny then. Now I 'ope yer satisfied.

MRS. PAR. (*kissing him*) There. *I* knew yer wouldn't act dishonourable. I knowed you better.

(*The door opens, the men come in, singing and laughing. ARTIE PEARCE crows like a cock. The GIRLS come down, hearing the noise*) Wot a time you people 'ave been.

MR. PAR. Wot 'a you been doin' all the time?

ARTIE. (*singing*) Making love in the evenin'
            Making love in the evenin'
A drop of zider sets one up like (*wiping his mouth*)

MRS. PAR. (*to Pargetter*) You'll 'ear later. All in good time. 'Ere Jenny, 'elp me with these chairs! I've watched it all right. Dick and you I mean. It's settled.

JENNY. (*with a chair*) Give I that one, Mother. O Mother, wot fun us shall 'ave.

MR. PAR. Now us be goin' to 'ave a dance.

A GIRL Be you a–goin' to dance, Mr. Pargetter?

MR. PAR. Course I be. Come, gaffer. Out with that fiddle o' yourn.

A GIRL. I do love a fiddle.

JENNY. A barrel hargin be good, too.

MR. PAR. Now, gaffer. Now, no long faces, anybody. Us be goin' to 'ave great times, ben't us?

NAN. Wait till I set thy chair right, gaffer.

GAFFER. (*querulously*) On the roads, I seen you. Surely. And it was all—all a–blowing?

NAN. Sit 'ere, now. And 'ave this cushion.

ARTIE. Don't let granfer fall into the fire. 'E will, if you don't watch it.

GAFFER. (*bowing in the old style*) Beauty makes women be proud. There be few beauties 'as the 'umbleness to 'elp a old man. Ah, there be no pleasure for the old; but to 'muse the young. I be a old man. A old, old man!

NAN. The old be wise, gaffer. The old 'ave peace, after their walking the world.

MRS. PAR. Stuff! (*a giggle*)

GAFFER. There be no peace to 'im as sees you, goin' by in beauty, puttin' fire to 'em.

GIRLS. Us be waitin'. Us be all ready!

MR. PAR. Take your—

GAFFER. (*to NAN*) What tune will the bride 'ave? A ring of bells and the maids flinging flowers at 'er. Like me and my girl 'ad. (*pause*) I 'ad a flower of 'er to go to church with. (*pause*) They put my flower under the mould after. (*pause*) I 'eard the mould go knock! (*he tunes his fiddle as he speaks*) No one remembers my white flower. (*pause*) That's sixty year ago.

NAN. You'll meet her again, gaffer. Per'aps she's by you now.

GAFFER. (*with a lifting voice—half rising*) So you've a come, my 'andsome—

MRS. PAR. 'Ere. (*she taps GAFFER'S hand*) Play! 'Ere! Fiddle. (*to NAN*) Don't you see you're upsettin' 'im. Move away. One'd think you'd no feelings.

MR. PAR. Take your partners.

MR. PAR. Now, 'ave you all got your partners?

ALL. No. Don't be so silly, Artie. Now, do be

quiet. 'Ow are us to dance! (*etc. etc.*) You come over 'ere, by me.

(*NAN stands a little apart, looking at DICK, waiting on him*)

MRS. PAR. Now, now, we're all 'ere. 'Ush a moment. Afore we begin there's a little bit o' noos just 'appened, as I'd like to say about.

ARTIE. 'Ear! 'Ear!

MR. PAR. (*to ARTIE*) You be quiet! (*He grins at ARTIE approvingly*)

MRS. PAR. As I'm sure 'll come as a great surprise. Really, it quite took my breath away! It did, really. Now, I mustn't stop you young people dancing. But I must just tell you this little bit of noos. He, he! Why—

ARTIE. We ain't lookin'.

A GIRL. Be quiet, Artie.

MRS. PAR. Jenny and Dick 'ere 'ave made a match of it. I 'ope the present company'll wish the 'appy couple joy! Dick! Jenny! Give me your 'ands. There. (*She clasps them*) I 'ope you'll be very 'appy together. Dick, (*kissing him*) you're my son now, ain't yer?

ARTIE. Spare 'is blushes, Mother.

ALL. Why, who'd ever a–thought it! I do 'ope you'll be 'appy. 'Ow sudden! Quite took my breath away! Jenny, come 'ere, and let I kiss 'ee. I s'pose us can't kiss you, Mr. Dick? No, Mr. Dick'll be quite the married man. 'E looks it already.

NAN. Dick, Dick, oh, Dick! What, oh, Dick, you weren't playing, Dick?

DICK. Don't Dick me. Get out!

MRS. PAR. Wot are yer bothering Dick for?

NAN. I thought 'e'd something—something to say to me.

46

DICK. You thought I was a oly scrawf, didn't yer?

NAN. I thought I was a 'appy woman, Dick. (*she looks at him and goes slowly over to a chair. As she goes*)

MR. PAR. Now, Nan. What are you waitin' for? Take your place 'ere and dance, now.

MRS. PAR. Per'aps Nan is like 'er father.

JENNY. (*sliding her feet about*) 'Ow's that, Mother?

MRS. PAR. Per'aps she can only dance on air.

NAN. (*going to her*) Yes, yes, I am like my father. You coward to say that.

MR. PAR. Wot are you thinking of, with company present?

MRS. PAR. You leave her to me. I'll deal with her. (*To the company*) She thought if she 'ad 'er 'air down an 'er neck un'ooked as *she* might 'ave a go in at Dick, 'ere.

TOMMY. 'Ope us didn't come too soon, Dick.

JENNY. She believes in giving all for love, Cousin Nan do.

MRS. PAR. She'll give no more in this house. Why, 'er dad was 'ung for a thief only last Christmas.

MR. PAR. Now, Mother, that's—No, she deserves it. She ain't been straight.

ALL. Ah.

NAN. Yes. I'd like you all to know that. My dad was 'ung at Glorster. I'd oughtn't to a shook your 'ands without I'd told you. I tried 'ard to tell you, Dick. Dick. Dick. I give you all I had. You 'ad me. Like I never was. Not to any. O Dick, I 'ope you'll be very, very 'appy.

DICK. 'Ere. Go and say your piece to Gaffer there. 'E 'asn't many pleasures, I've done with yer. 'Ere, Jenny, you be goin' to dance with I.

47

JENNY. (*giggling*) I think I could 'elp, Dick Gurvil.

DICK. 'Elp me then. Come on.

JENNY. Law. It make my heart all of a flower. That's wot Cousin Nan says. I s'pose it must be very clever if 'er says it.

NAN. I wish—I wish the grass was over my 'ed.

DICK. 'Ere. Us wish to dance.

(NAN *goes aside*)

GAFFER. A bride's tears be zoon a–dried. But love be a zweet vlower. A girt red vlower. Her do last for ever. For ever. (*He plays "Joan to the Maypole"*) Like me and my girl, for ever!

(*They dance*)

CURTAIN

ACT III

(SCENE:—The same. NAN at table at back. A noise within. GAFFER in his chair)

NAN. Life be that bitter. O dad, life be that bitter.

GAFFER. You be young to 'ave life bitter on you.

NAN. It isn't time makes us old.

GAFFER. Some on us is glad to go away. Quite early.

NAN. I wish I could go away. I wish I could go away.

GAFFER. Us'll all be took away, afore long.

NAN. I'd like to be took away now.

GAFFER. I've a–wanted to be took away ever since my vlower were took. Many a long year. And I grawed to be a old, old man. I were out of work sometimes. And I be old now. Very old.

NAN. Per'aps you'll join 'er soon, gaffer.

GAFFER. Noa. Not for a girt while. I 'ave 'er little grave. I 'ave 'er little grave to see to. With vlowers and that. If I 'ad girt bags of gold like Squire, I could 'ave a 'edstone put. I'd 'ave 'er little grave all carved. I'd 'ave posies cut. And 'er face down on the stone. All in white I'd 'ave my vlower cut. White stone. There be no kings 'd 'ave whiter. But I can't never avord a 'edstone. So I ben't goin' to die. Noa. I ben't goin' to die.

49

NAN. When love be dead, gaffer, what be there else?

GAFFER. There be the grave. It be all the poor 'as, just the grave. And I got my vlower's grave. Eight maids in white there was. No older than my vlower they was. And there were all white vlowers on 'er. Eight maids in white, maidy. And the bell tolling. Oh, my white blossom to go under the grass.

NAN. She was very young to be took, Gaffer.

GAFFER. They was eight maids in white when they carried 'er. Then they was women. Beautiful they were. Then they grew old. One by one. And then their 'ouses were to let, with the windows broke. And grass and grass. They be all gone. When I be gone there'll be none to tell the beauty of my vlower. There'll be none as knows where 'er body lies. I 'ave 'er little grave all done with shells. And the vlowers that do come up, they be little words from 'er. Little zhining words. Fifty-nine year them little words come.

NAN. I got a grave, too, gaffer. And I 'ave fifty-nine years to come.

GAFFER. My bright 'ansome. Oo 'ave you in yer grave?

NAN. I 'ave my 'eart in the grave, gaffer. But there'll be no vlowers come up out of 'er. I shall be 'ere fifty-nine year per'aps. Like you been. Fifty-nine year. Twelve times fifty-nine is—and four times that. Three hundred and sixty-five days in a year. Up, and work, and lie down again. But dead, dead, dead. All the time dead. No. No. Not that. Gaffer. How did thy vlower die?

GAFFER. There come a gold rider in the evening, maidy.

NAN. You was by 'er, Gaffer?

GAFFER. She look out of the window, my white vlower done. She said, "The tide. The tide. The tide coming up the river". And a horn blew. The gold rider blew a 'orn. And she rose up, my white vlower done. And she burst out a–laughing, a–laughing. And 'er fell back, my white vlower done. Gold 'air on the pillow. And blood. Oh, blood. Blood of my girl. Blood of my vlower.

NAN. In your arms, gaffer?

GAFFER. On my 'eart. My white vlower lay on my 'eart. The tide. The tide. The tide coming up the river.

NAN. She was 'appy to die so, gaffer. Along of 'er true love. You 'ad the sweet of love along of your vlower. But them as 'as the sharp of love. Them as never 'as no sweet. O I wish the tide was comin' up over my 'ed, I do.

GAFFER. It be full moon to–night, maidy.

NAN. Full moon. It come up misty. And red.

GAFFER. It was red on the pillow. Then.

NAN. The harvest–moon.

GAFFER. There'll be a high tide to–night.

NAN. A high tide.

GAFFER. For some on us.

NAN. Why for some on us, gaffer?

GAFFER. The tide be comin' for some on us.

NAN. For you, gaffer?

GAFFER. Ther've come no message yet for me. But the tide be a'comin' for some on us. It 'ave someone every time. It 'ad my vlower one time. O it be a gallows thing, the tide. First there be the mud and that. Sand banks. Mud banks. And the 'erons fishing. Sand in the river, afore the tide comes. Mud. The cows come out o' pasture to drink. They come on the sand. Red cows. But they be afraid of the tide.

51

NAN. They 'aven't no grief, the beasts asn't. Cropping in the meadows when the sun do zhine.

GAFFER. They be afraid of the tide. For first there come a–wammerin' and a–wammerin'. Miles away that wammerin' be. In the sea. The shipmen do cross theirselves. And it come up. It come nearer. Wammerin' Wammerin'! 'Ush it says. 'Ush it says. 'Ush it says. And there come a girt wash of it over the rock. White. White. Like a bird. Like a swan a-gettin' up out of the pool.

NAN. Bright it goes. High. High up. Flashing.

GAFFER. And it wammers and it bubbles. And then it spreads. It goes out like soldiers. It go out into a line. It curls. It curls. It go toppling and toppling. And on it come. And on it come.

NAN. Fast. Fast.

A black line. And the foam all creamin' on it.

GAFFER. It be a snake. A snake. A girt water snake with its 'ed up. Swimming. On it come.

NAN. A bright crown upon it. And hungry.

GAFFER. With a rush. With a roar. And its claws clutchin' at you. Out they go at the sides, the claws do.

NAN. The claws of the tide.

GAFFER. Singing. Singing. And the sea a-roaring after. O, it takes them. They stand out in the river. And it goes over them. Over them. Over them. One roarin' rush.

NAN. Deep. Deep. Water in their eyes. Over their hair. And to-night it be the harvest tide.

GAFFER. (*as though waking from a dream*) The salmon-fishers 'll lose their nets to-night.

The tide'll sweep them away. O, I've known it. It takes the nets up miles. Miles. They find 'em high up. Beyond Glorster. Beyond 'Artpury. Girt golden flag-flowers over 'em. And appletrees a-growin' over 'em. Apples of red and apples of gold. They fall into the water. The water be still there, where the apples fall. The nets 'ave apples in them.

NAN. And fish, gaffer?

GAFFER. Strange fish. Strange fish out of the sea.

NAN. Yes. Strange fish indeed, gaffer. A strange fish in the nets to-morrow. A dumb thing. Knocking agen the bridges. Something white. Something white in the water. They'd pull me out. Men would. They'd touch my body. (*shuddering*) I couldn't. I couldn't.

(*Loud laughter from within, and a clatter of knives. The door opens. ENTER JENNY from inner room, carrying a dirty plate, with dirty knife and fork. As JENNY comes in, MRS. PARGETTER is heard off*)

MRS. PAR. Is *she* in there?

JENNY. Yes.

MRS. P. Tell 'er to come in.

JENNY. (*to NAN*) You're to go in, mother says.

PAR. (*heard off*) 'Ere, shut that door behind yer. It blows my 'ed off. (*JENNY turns and shuts the door*)

NAN. What 'ave you got there, Jenny?

JENNY. (*uneasily*) You're to go in, mother says.

NAN. (*rising*) Never mind what mother says. Answer my question, my friend, my girt friend, my little creeping friend. What 'ave you got there?

JENNY. (*shrinking*) A mutton parsty pie for gaffer, as mother sent. It'll be a little treat for 'im.

NAN. (*looking*) Whose plate have you brought it on, my little friend?

53

JENNY. (*stammering*) Mother's plate.

NAN. It is a dirty plate. And the knives and forks are dirty.

JENNY. (*confidently*) Gaffer won't know any different. It's good enough for an old man like 'im. 'Ere, gaffer. 'Ere's some supper for yer.

NAN. (*going up to her*) No, my friend, my girt friend, my little Judas friend, my little pale snake friend. It's not good enough. Did *you* 'ave one of them pies?

JENNY. (*blustering*) You can—I ain't goin' to—

NAN. Did you? The sheep died. The sheep died last week. Did *you* eat one of them pies?

JENNY. No, I know what the sheep die of. Gaffer won't mind. 'Ere, gaffer.

NAN. (*fiercely*) Sit down, my little friend. Sit down and eat that pie yourself. Eat it. Eat it or I'll kill you. Eat it. You with no charity to old or young. You shall eat the charity of the uncharitable. Eat it. You little snake. Eat it.

JENNY. I'll—I'll send mother to you.

NAN. (*preventing her*) No. Oh, no. (*forcing her into a chair*) Eat. Eat. (*JENNY in great terror begins to eat*)

JENNY. I be goin' to be sick.

NAN. Eat. (*JENNY eats. Then shrinks back*)

JENNY. (*after a mouthful*) Wot are you lookin' at me for?

NAN. I'm looking at my friend. My friend.

JENNY. (*after a mouthful*) I can't eat with you watchin me.

NAN. Yes, Jenny. It is your bride cake. Your bride cake. Your bride cake for your marriage, Jenny.

JENNY. (*screaming*) *Don't* look at me like that.

54

NAN. (*coming up to her and glaring down into her face*) Yes, Jenny. I must look at you like this. I must look into your soul, Jenny. Into your soul. (*Slowly and quietly*)

JENNY. Ah-h.

NAN. You 'ave pale eyes, Jenny. Pale eyes. I can look into your soul. D'you know what I see, Jenny? (*a pause*) I see your soul. It is cold, Jenny. It's a little mean cold, lying thing. You're a lucky one, Jenny. You cannot love nor hate. A dog loves more and hates more. A worm do. D'you know what comes to such souls, Jenny?

JENNY. (*gasping*) Mother! Mother!

NAN. I'll tell you, Jenny. I'll tell your future to you. I see your life very plain in your pale eyes. I see a girt town, with lamps. And I see you in a public 'ouse, Jenny, with red on your white cheeks. And your pale eyes are swollen with drink. And you've a raggy skirt And you cough. And you tremble. That is the pay in this world, Jenny, for a little cold mean lying thing. And I see a dirty room with a dirty bed, and you lying dead on it. Your painted cheeks on the pillow. Till the town dead-cart come. Out with you. Out with you. Out with you. (*JENNY totters, gasping, to the door*)

JENNY. Ah. Ah-h! (*she leans up against the door, holding it by the latch, in terror; she is only half conscious*)

GAFFER. (*rousing and shading his eyes looking up*) Be you ready for your journey, maidy?

NAN. My journey.

GAFFER. You must eat and drink, my 'andsome. 'E be coming.

NAN. Who be coming?

GAFFER. The gold rider, maidy. 'E be comin' on the road.

55

NAN. The gold rider. We will eat and drink, gaffer. It be a long road to go. (*She opens oven and brings out the apple-pasty; then takes a carving knife, and plate. Then the brandy bottle. She cuts the pasty and gives food to GAFFER*)

GAFFER. (*rising unsteadily and holding up his hands*) Bless this food to thy service. Bless the Giver of all good things. Amen. (*He eats.*)

NAN. Amen. (*The outer door is knocked. Footsteps outside*) Drink, gaffer. (*She gives him a sup of brandy*)

GAFFER. (*drinking to her*) A fair journey. Vlowers on the road afore you. O gold 'oofs. Gold 'oofs. Be swift. Swift. (*A knocking at outer door*)

A VOICE. Is anyone inside there? Open.

NAN. Drink, gaffer. (*Violent knocking outside. The inner door is shaken by those within. JENNY holds the latch and keeps them from entering*)

JENNY. O! O! Don't let 'er in on me. Don't let 'er in on me. (*Falling against the wall*) Oh, oh.

(*ENTER the PARGETTERS and DICK. The others cluster at the doorway*)

DICK. (*seeing JENNY and glad to have NAN for once in the wrong. Angrily*) Wot 'ave you been doin' to 'er? Eh?

MRS. PAR. (*advancing on NAN*) Why can't you open the door? Standing staring there.

PAR. Wot 'ave she done to you, Jenny?

MRS. PAR. (*turning*) Never you 'eed wot she's done to 'er. You go and open the door. 'Ere, Jenny. Go on inside. Go on now. Before they see yer.

DICK. She's—she's—Best 'ave 'er locked up, mother.

MRS. PAR. Open the door, there.

(*JENNY totters out*)

MR. PAR. Wot's brought 'er into that state?

56

NAN. She has seen herself, uncle. There's few can bear that sight. A worm in the dust fears it.

MRS. P. You don't mean to say as you've cut the parsty.

PAR. 'Ush. They'll 'ear yer.

MRS. P. (*in a blood-curdling voice*) And look at your uncle's bottle. If I don't give it yer for this. (*A knock*)

A VOICE WITHOUT. Come on. Come on. I've got no time to waste.

MRS. P. (*going to the door with her best society smile*) I didn't 'ear yer knock. Wot with comp'ny. I 'ope I aven't kep you waitin', I'm sure. (*peering at visitors*) Good evenin', sir. Will, fetch chairs for the gentlemen. Why, it's Mr. Drew. Come in, sir. Won't you please ter come in, sir.

DREW. Thank you.

(*ENTER PARSON DREW, CAPTAIN DIXON and a CONSTABLE carrying a hand bag*)

PAR. (*fetching chairs*) Good evenin', sir.

DREW. Good evenin', Pargetter.

PAR. (*to DIXON*) Good evenin', sir.

DIXON. (*coldly to CONSTABLE*) Put that bag on the table.

DREW. Well, Dick. Is that you, Ellen? You grow so fast. Nan. Yes. Yes. Good evening, everybody.

PAR. (*in a stage whisper to MRS. PARGETTER*) 'Ave the table cleared.

DIXON. (*irritably*) Never mind the table.

MRS. PAR. You must excuse things bein' a bit untidy, sir. Wot with 'avin company, we're all topsy turvy, as you mid say. (*suavely to NAN*) Jest take that parsty off the table, Nan, there's a good girl.

NAN. I've done with make-believes, Aunt. One makes believe too long.

57

MRS. P. (*to DREW*) She loves a bit of play-actin', sir. She do it wonderful, considerin'.

DIXON. Oh, Drew. Drew. (*Irritably*)

MRS. P. She's been givin' us a bit out of Shakespeare as they call it.

DREW. Yes. Yes. Yes. Now hush, please, a moment everybody. (*EVERYBODY is silent*) (*Raising a hand*) I'm afraid we come at a very inconvenient time. But—(*seeing those in the door*) Oh, just come in there, will you? Yes. Yes. It's a very pleasant duty. It's not often that I have such a pleasure as I have to-night. (*taking chair*) Yes. Thank you. Sit down, Mr. Dixon.

DIXON. (*coldly*) *Captain* Dixon.

DREW. Yes, yes, to be sure. Captain Dixon, to be sure. I beg your pardon, Captain Dixon. I'm sure you'll all be very glad when you hear what it is that makes us interrupt your evening's pleasure.

DIXON. (*tartly*) Excuse me, Mr. Drew. But hadn't we better come to business?

DREW. Yes, yes, but—

DIXON. (*mildly*) I shall miss the coach back to town.

DREW. O, no, no, no, no. O, no, no, no. Oh, you've ten minutes yet. More. You've got lots of time. You'll hear the horn long before the coach is due.

MRS. P. Yes, sir. You'll 'ear the horn a long ways off. If it's the coach you want.

GAFFER. The horn. The horn. Gold hoofs beating on the road. (*he advances to the table*) They beat like the ticking of a 'eart. Soon. Very soon. The golden trump.

MRS. P. (*angrily*) Could ever anything! (*quietly*) You old stupe. Take 'im out, Will. Don't let 'im begin in 'ere. (*to Dixon*) Don't mind 'im, sir. 'E's silly.

(*GAFFER goes to the door and looks out into the moonlight*)

GAFFER. (*at the door*) Maybe I'll meet 'im on the road.

(*He goes out*)

DREW. One of our—You know, eh. (*taps his forehead*)

DIXON. (*sourly*) I thought it was another bit out of Shakespeare as they call it.

PAR. Yes, sir. 'E talks very strange sometimes.

DREW. Yes, yes, poor fellow.

DIXON. I suppose this is the right house?

DREW. Yes, of course. Yes, certainly, certainly.

DIXON. (*taking bag and unlocking it*) I thought it might be the—the—Yes. Ye-es. Very well, then. (*suddenly*) Which of you is Nan Hardwick?

NAN. I am that one.

DIXON. Ye-es. You. Very well then. Is that correct, Mr. Drew?

DREW. Certainly. Certainly.

DIXON. Daughter of Mary Hardwick, and of—of Edward Hardwick who was—eh?

NAN. Who was hanged at Gloucester.

DIXON. Of Swanscombe, in the Hundred of—Yes. Very well then. (*turning to others*) You certify that this is that Nan Hardwick?

THE OTHERS. Yes, sir. That be 'er.

DIXON. Very well, then. That's not the horn, Drew?

DREW. O, no, no.

DIXON. (*taking bag and papers out of handbag*) Have you a pen and ink in the house?

PAR. (*taking them from the dresser*) This is a pen and ink, sir.

59

DIXON. Ye-es. (*writes*) This pen's—Drew, have
you got a pen? (*to MRS. PAR.*) Give me a pen-
wiper. (*he wipes, and then mends pen with a pen-
knife*) Ye-es. Ye-es. (*sharply*) Nan Hardwick,
your father was—er—put to death for stealing a sheep
near Aston Magna. No. Don't answer. That
is the fact. Ye-es. Very well then. The sheep
was the property of Mr. Nicols. Now it has been
proved that your father, Edward Hardwick, had
nothing to do with that sheep.

NAN. And you come here, do you, to tell me that?
You have a thousand men beneath you, a thousand
strong men like the man there. And you have
judges in scarlet, and lawyers in wigs. And a little
child out of the road could have told you that my dad
was innocent. A little child of the road. By once
looking in his eyes.

DIXON. I can't go into all that. You must keep to
the point. (*DREW whispers*) What? Yes. Yes.
I daresay.

DREW. (*to NAN*) Let Captain Dixon finish
what he's got to say.

MRS P. Where's yer manners gorn? You wait
till afterwards.

DIXON. To continue. The sheep was stolen by
Mr Nicol's shepherd, who was the chief witness
against your father.

NAN. The sheep was stolen by Richard Shapland.

DIXON. (*staring at her*) Who has since confessed.

ALL. Ah. Confessed. Think of that. There
now.

DIXON. A sad miscarriage of justice. Very well
then. While we support the laws, we must be con-
tent to suffer from their occasional misapplication.
(*glances at his watch*)

DREW. Lots of time. Lots of time.

60

DIXON. Ye-es. But in this instance, the Home Office has decided to offer you some compensation.

NAN. Some blood-money. Thirty pieces of silver.

DIXON. No. It's more. It's fifty pounds. (*he empties bag*) Will you count it over please, before signing the receipt?

NAN. No. No. The blood and tears are sticky on it.

DREW. She's upset. I'll count it.

PAR. (*pouring brandy for NAN*) 'Ere, Nan. 'Ave just a drop.

(*She refuses*)

OTHERS. Fifty pou-und. Fifty pou-und. Did you ever.

DICK. (*muttering*) A 'orse and trap. And furnish a 'ouse.

DREW. Fifty. Would you like to count it over, Pargetter?

PAR. No, thanky, sir, I'm sure.

DIXON. (*to NAN*) Are you satisfied? (*sharply*) Nan Hardwick.

NAN. What d'you want more?

DIXON. Are you satisfied that the sum is correct?

NAN. Oh. The money. You know it is. Why go to all this trouble? Give me your pen. There. There's my name to your paper. Received. By me. Fifty pounds in gold.

DIXON. And the date. Ye-es. I'll just add the date. (*to the CONSTABLE*) Witness it, Horton. (*the man signs. He looks at his watch again*) I shall miss that coach.

DREW. Won't you think better of it, and stay the night? Stay, man, stay and see the tide. It's a wonderful sight.

DIXON. No, thanks. No, thanks. (*he gathers up his handbag*) Here you are, Horton. (*Gives him*

61

bag) I hope the money may be a comfort to you. (*to NAN*) Where can I catch this coach?

MRS P. Just down the lane, sir. It is but a step. Keep on right down, sir. You can't miss it, sir.

PAR. You'll 'ear the 'arn go, sir.

DIXON AND HORTON. Good night. (*going*)

ALL. Good night, sir. Good night, Officer.

DICK. (*to PARGETTER*) Wouldn't 'e take a drop of somethin'?

PAR. Noa. It's not for the likes of us to offer.

DICK. You can't ever tell.

DREW. I'm sure that what we have just heard has given us all a great deal of pleasure. I won't dwell on the satisfaction to yourself, Nan, for fear of giving you pain. But I am sure that your good aunt, who has been so kind to you—

MRS P. No more than my sacred dooty, Mr. Drew.

DREW. (*gallantly*) I will spare your blushes, Mrs. Pargetter. And all your young friends who are here to-night. I'm sure that they all feel with me—

(*RE-ENTER DIXON*)

DIXON. Excuse me, Drew. Do show me the way to where the coach passes. These beastly lanes are—

DREW. Yes. Yes. Certainly. Certainly. (*to the Company*) I must wish you all good night. So sorry to have interrupted your evening's amusement.

MRS P. A pleasure I'm sure, sir.

DREW. (*to NAN*) By the way, Nan. Perhaps I should say Miss Hardwick, now you're an heiress. Mrs. Drew would like to see you at the Rectory to-morrow—She thinks you might like to live with us as our housekeeper.

DIXON. Come on. Come on.

DREW. Coming, Captain Dixon. But we'll go into that to-morrow. Shall we?

NAN. Thank you, sir. I hope you'll thank Mrs.

Drew, too, sir. But I shall not come to the Rectory
to-morrow. Unless—Unless the fishers bring their
take to you. For you to choose your tithe.

DREW. (*puzzled*) Well. Ah. Ah yes. Well,
think it over. Sleep on it.

NAN. I shall sleep soundly on it.

DREW. Good night, everybody. Now. Captain
Dixon.

(*EXIT*)

(*returning*) Mrs Pargetter!

MRS P. Yes, sir. (*He draws her aside and whispers, pointing to NAN*)

DREW. (*in stage whisper*) To bed at once.

(*NAN smiles bitterly*)

MRS P. Yes, sir. Pore thing, it's been too much
for 'er. I don't wonder.

(*EXIT DREW*)

MRS P. 'E's gone at last. (*to the others*) Go on
in back to supper. Us'll be with yer in a minute.
Shut the door. There's sech a draught.

(*They go*)

DICK. I'll fetch in Miss Nan a bit of supper.

MRS P. It's a pity you don't 'eed the mote in yer
own eye without 'eedin' the camel in yer neighbour's.
Go in and see to Jenny.

PAR. Well, Nan, it be a long lane as 'as no turning, as they say. I knew thy pore dad when us was
boys. When us goe'd a nesting after ardiestraws.
Dear, dear. 'E won the prize for kiddy potatoes,
and for kiddy beans. I be glad, that I be, to 'ear—
wot we've 'eard to-night.

NAN. So you are glad, are you? Glad.

MRS P. If you 'adn't a black 'eart, you'd be glad
yourself, I should a-thought. Some people a-got no
feelin's.

PAR. Fifty pound be a lot of money, too.

NAN. The worth of a man's life 'ad need to be a lot of money.

PAR. There's two things you could do with all that money. You could put er into the Bank and that. Or you could—I'd be very glad to borrow it of you, to 'elp me on the farm. And pay you the interest, like.

NAN. And if I'd refuse. What then?

MRS. P. Refuse? Refuse? I don't doubt you give yerself airs. It's wot we'd expect of yer—

PAR. (*interrupting*) I'm only asking.—To keep it in the family.

MRS P. (*to PAR.*) Asking? Givin' in to |'er wills and 'er won'ts. Wot's asking got to do with it? 'Ere. You're under age. We're yer guardians. *We'll* take care of that money for yer.

NAN. Yes. You'll want some money, for Jenny's portion.

PAR. (*controlling his temper*) I 'aven't said nothink yet—

MRS P. No. You 'aven't got the sperrit of a 'og with the twitters.

PAR. (*angrily*) I don't want none of *yer* jaw.

MRS P. Don't you nag at me, for I won't 'ave it. See?

NAN. The money is mine. Not yours. I have a use for it.

PAR. (*to NAN*) Then I've done with yer. You talk rude to the quality. You give all sorts of talk to—Talk as 'd sick a savage. Do wot y' like with yer money. But you'll make good my Toby jug, at least. Now then.

NAN. Your Toby jug?

PAR. You know wot I mean.

NAN. Aha. The little friend. My little friend.

64

(*a cry within*)   That's 'er soul's voice that cry is.   So *that* is wot—

MRS P.   And you 'ad the cold blooded cheek to 'ave your go at the parsty, wot's more.

PAR.   And—there—I'll leave you to your conscience.   (*going*)

MRS P.   Stop a moment, Will.   Us'll settle 'er with 'er, onst for all.

NAN.   (*going to the money bag and cutting its tape*) Yes.   We'll settle.   Look at it.   Look at it.   (*she pours the gold into a heap*)   Gold.   Gold.   Little yellow rounds of metal.   Fifty little yellow rounds of metal.   This.   This is for a man's life.   Oh, you little yellow rounds that buy things.   Look at 'em. Hear 'em.   (*pause*)   Don't you speak to me.   (*intensely*)   There was a strong man, a kind man.   He was forty-nine years old.   He was the best thatcher in the three counties.   He was the sweetest singer. I've known teams goin' to the field stop to 'ear my dad sing.   And the red coats come.   And a liar swore. And that strong man was killed.   Sudden.   That voice of his'n was choked out with a cord.   And there was liars, and thieves, and drunken women, and dirty gentlemen.   They all stood in the cold to see that man choked.   They stop up all night, playing cards, so as they should 'ear 'is singin' stopped.   For it goes round the voice the cord do.   And they draw a nightcap down so as 'e shan't see 'is girl a-crying. (*pause*)   And for that, I get little yellow round things.   (*pause*)   And there was a girl, a young girl, a girl with a sick 'eart.   D'you know what came to 'er?   You know what came to 'er.   She came among them as might have made much of 'er. For she'd 'ave give a lot for a kind word.   'Er 'eart was that broke 'er'd 'ave broke out a-crying at a kind word.

65

MRS P. When you've done with your fal-lals, I'll 'ave my say.

NAN. Don't you speak. Don't you threaten. You'll listen to me. You 'ad me in your power. And wot was good in me you sneered at. And wot was sweet in me, you soured. And wot was bright in me you dulled. I was a fly in the spider's web. And the web came round me and round me, till it was a shroud, till there was no more joy in the world. Till my 'eart was bitter as that ink, and all choked. And for that I get little yellow round things. (*pause and change of voice*) And all of it—No need for any of it. My dad's life, and your taunts, and my broke 'eart. All a mistake. A mistake. Somethin' to be put right by fifty pound while a gentleman waits for a coach. 'E thought nothing of it. 'E thought only of getting the coach. 'Ed didn't even pretend. (*a cry within*) It were a game to 'im. 'E laughed at it. (*a cry within*) Yes. She has seen herself. No wonder she cries. She sees the parish dead-cart coming.

(*DICK puts his head in at the door*)

DICK. Mother. Come to Jenny. Quick.

MRS P. To 'ell with Jenny. I've somethin' to attend to 'ere.

DICK. She's in a fit or somethink. Us can 'ardly 'old 'er down.

MRS P. (*to NAN*) More of yer work. You wait till I come back.

A GIRL. (*at the door*) Quick, Mrs Pargetter.

(*MRS PARGETTER snatches the brandy bottle and goes out*)

PAR. I don't know 'ow all this'll end, Nan.

(*He goes out*)

(*RE-ENTER DICK*)

DICK. I brought you a little bit o' supper, Miss Nan.

66

NAN. What then?

DICK I thought—Won't you sit down and 'ave it, Miss Nan? There. Let me put this chair comferable.

NAN. Why do you bring this to me?

DICK. I thought—some'ow—I thought you'd like a bit of cossitin'.

NAN. I want nothin'. Nothin'.

DICK Miss Nan. I want just to say. Some 'ow, it be 'ard to explain. But I ask—I ask your forgiveness. 'Umbly I ask it. Oh, Miss Nan. My beauti-vul. My beautivul as I wronged.

NAN. As you wronged. Yes?

DICK. I was—I dunno—I was led away, Miss Nan.

NAN. Yes, Dick. You were led away. How were you led away? Why?

DICK. I was that. When I 'eard as your dad was. I mean when I 'eard of your dad. I doan' know. It seemed—I felt some'ow. I be that dry I can't 'ardly speak. Miss Nan—

NAN. You felt some'ow? Yes?

DICK. As your 'air was, was a cord round my throat. Choking. I was sick. I couldn't—no—I couldn't.

NAN. And was that the only reason why?

DICK. Yes, Miss Nan.

NAN. And why did you choose Jenny? My kiss was still warm upon your lips. (*going to him*) Your blood was singing in your veins with me, when you turned—Why did you turn to 'er?
(*a pause*)
She was not a—a gallus-bird. Eh?
(*A pause. DICK licks his lips and swallows*)
(*RE-ENTER GAFFER slowly, with a few roses plucked in the garden. He goes to NAN*)

67

GAFFER. The moon be at full, O wonder. The cows in the meadows kneel down.

The rabbits be kneelin'. The vlowers in the edge do kneel—

Roses for your 'air, my beauty. O my bright 'ansome of the world.

(*He gives the roses reverently*)

Roses in your 'air. And the bride's 'air loose.

(*NAN places a rose in her hair and loosens it about her*)

NAN. (*taking some money*) For a 'eadstone, Gaffer. (*sharply*) Well, Dick.

DICK. I was.—O, I can't. To show that I 'ad done with yer. I was angry.

NAN. Because I didn't tell you of my dad?

DICK. Yes.

NAN. There be three times, Dick, when no woman can speak. Beautiful times. When 'er 'ears 'er lover, and when 'er gives 'erself, and when 'er little one is born. You—You'd have been the first to stop me if I'd spoken then.

DICK. I thought as you'd—not been straight—I thought—

NAN. And now you turn again from Jenny. Why have you left Jenny, Dick?

GAFFER. (*jangling and counting money*)

'Nine. 'Ow the bells do chime,

'Ten. There's a path for men.'

DICK. Because I don't care for 'er. Because now—

GAFFER. 'Leven. From the earth to 'eaven.

DICK. Be quiet, Gaffer.

NAN. Because?

DICK. O, Miss Nan. It be you as I love. My dad 'ave stop me afore. But now your name be cleared—

NAN. Is that the only reason?

GAFFER. (*talking through*) Twelve. Twelve. Us rang out a peal at twelve. Angels. Gold angels. The devil walks the dark at twelve. Ghosts. Ghosts. Behind the white 'edstones. Smite 'em, gold rider. Smite 'em with thy bright sharp spear.

NAN. Is that the only reason? You love me, then?

DICK. Yes. That's the only reason. I love you, Nan.

NAN. And what will my aunt say?

DICK. Damn 'er. It's 'er that came between us.

NAN. I know what you can say to 'er.

DICK. What?

NAN. Go to her now. Take her that bag of money. Tell her she may have that. But that you will marry me, not Jenny.

(*DICK, rather staggered, takes up the bag and walks slowly to door*)

DICK. Wouldn't it be better, Miss Nan, if us—if us just told 'er, without—without bein'—

NAN. I knew it. I knew it.

(*A horn is heard faintly off*)

GAFFER. There be a music on the sea, a soft music. The ships be troubled at the music.

NAN. Come here, Dick. They said my dad kill a sheep. A foundered old ewe as'd feel nothin'; 'ardly the knife on 'er throat. And my dad was 'ung; only acos they said 'e kill a beast like that. They choked 'im dead, in front of 'alf a city. But you come. And you 'ave yer love of a girl. You says lovely things to 'er. Things as'd move any girl—and only because you be greedy. Greedy of a mouth agen your mouth; of a girl's lips babblin' love at you. And a sour old woman's word'll make you 'it that girl across the lips you kissed. In ten minutes. You'll

69

take 'er lovin' 'eart and 'er girl's pride, and all 'er joy
in the world, and stamp it in the dust. And you'll
dance on 'er white body; and all you'll feel is the
blood makin' a mess on your boots.

(*The horn blows nearer*)

GAFFER. The horn. The horn. O night owl
laughing in the wood.

NAN And you go to another girl. And you give
'er a joy in the world. And then you see your old
love not wot the old woman said. No. But as sweet
to the taste, as dear to your greedy mouth. And with
gold—yellow round things—to buy vanity. 'Ouses,
'orses, position. Then you come back whining.
Whining! For 'er to take you back. So as you mid
'ave that gold.

DICK. O, you can talk. You've a right. But I
love you, Nan. I do love yer.

NAN. I see very plain to-night, Dick. I see right,
right into you. Right down. You talk o' thieves.
You talk o' them as kills—them as leads women
wrong. Sinners you calls them. But it be you is the
sinner. You kill people's 'earts. You stamp them
in the dust, like worms as you tread on in the fields.
And under it all will be the women crying, the broken
women, the women cast aside. Tramped on. Spat
on. As you spat on me. No, no, oh no. Oh young
man in your beauty—Young man in your strong hun-
ger. I will spare those women.

DICK. (*scared, and speaking loudly, so as to attract
them in the inner room*) I never! Mother! Mother!

GAFFER. O Love you be a King. A King.

NAN. I will spare those women. Come here to me.

DICK. Ah! Ah! Mother! (*he backs towards the
door*)

GAFFER. On the road. They come. Gold hoofs.
Gold hoofs.

70

NAN. Spare them. Spare them. Spare them the hell. The hell of the heart-broken. Die—you—die. (*she stabs him with the pastry knife. He falls*)

DICK. (*raising himself stupidly*) The drums be a-roaring. A-roaring. (*he dies*)

GAFFER. (*clapping his hands*) Oh Beauty, beauty. Oh beauty of my white vlower.

(*A murmuring and rushing noise is heard as the tide sweeps up from the sea*)

GAFFER. (*shouts*) It be coming. Out of the wells of the sea. The eagles of the sea hear it. They sharp their beaks.

(*ENTER hurriedly the others*)

MRS P. (*running to DICK*) Dick. Dick. Oh! (*screams*) Look at it all smoking.

PAR. 'Ere. The brandy. Quick. 'E's gone.

NAN. (*as the noise increases*) The tide.

GAFFER. The tide.

NAN. (*laughing*) The tide coming up the river.

MRS P. Take the money, Will. Don't 'eed the brandy.

A GIRL. The pleece, Artie. Get the pleece.

NAN. (*going to the door as the noise increases*) A strange fish in the nets to-morrow

(*She goes*)

GAFFER. Singing. Singing. Roaring it come. Roaring it come. Over the breast. Over the lips. Over the eyes.

(*The horn blows*)

MRS P. (*putting the money hastily in the locker*) That's something. Wot are we to tell them?

(*The coach-horn blows loudly and clearly*)

GAFFER. The horn! The horn!

CURTAIN

71

THE CAMPDEN WONDER

THE CAMPDEN WONDER

PERSONS

	PLAYED BY
JOHN PERRY . . .	Mr. Norman McKinnel
DICK PERRY . . .	Mr. H. R. Hignett
PARSON	Mr. Edmund Gurney
TOM CONSTABLE . . .	Mr. Norman Page
MRS. PERRY . . .	Miss Carlotta Addison
MRS. HARRISON . .	Miss Dolores Drummond

This play was produced at the Court Theatre, in London, on the 8th of January, 1907, under the direction of Mr. H. Granville Barker.

THE CAMPDEN WONDER

SCENE. *Harrison's Kitchen in Campden.*

JOAN: Be the master come home from Charringworth yet?

RICH: I an't heard him, I an't.

JOAN: He be gone a great while. It's near ten.

RICH: (*going to the door*) Be you there, Master?—No, a ben't come home yet, Mother.

JOAN: Why, whatever have a kept 'en. If that ben't ten a striking!

RICH: Old Mr Curtis, he've a harvest feast tonight. Her'll have stopped with old Mr Curtis, Mother. Her'll sleep there after veast, in the barn, I do think.

JOAN: (*laughing*) He be a good one, he be. Seventy year old he be—And her do drink, her do, and her do sing. Law! how a do sing, to be sure; and a do like a's ale.

RICH: Her be a good old soul—A old ram, he be. Lor, now, to think on the merry deeds of him, the old sinful soul. Only last year now—him away so sly now, like a old fox. They said a was killed for sure; and there a were to Gloucester surely, a drinking, a drinking merry, and him his threescore and ten!

JOAN: Her be a merry old soul. Her be a trusty good soul—And a be a good master. Her've done right by thee, Dick.

RICH: Her did say this noon, I should have twelve

77

shillin' a week after Michaelmas. That's more than brother John gets.

JOAN: Ah, to think of that now! More than thy brother John! Thy brother John—he be a strange one, he be. I do fear I'll live to see thy brother John hanged! He be earnin' nine shillin' a week, and he drink that, he do.—And he be a handsome lad, Dick, a fine grown lad, John be. He be like his feyther was.

RICH: I do think as how a should do summat for you, Mother, and not go a-drinking all he do earn.

JOAN: He be a handsome lad, Dick, thy brother John. A dear, a dear, he be the very spit of his poor feyther, and he be a sad one, he be; and he do drink all his nine shillin'.

(ENTER JOHN)

JOHN: Who do drink all his nine shillin'?

JOAN: Ah, John! there thou be, lad. You be late out, John.

JOHN: You were talking about me, you were. You were saying as I drank—you and Dick there. He be a godly one, brother Dick be. (*To DICK*) You keep your tongue shut about me, and about my nine shillin'. If I do drink it, I drink it open. I ben't one to go knucklin' to pa'son, I ben't. Nor I don't go knucklin' to my lord, like some I know.

JOAN: There, there, John. Don't 'ee take on, now!

RICH: It would be better, I do think, if as how you did go knucklin', as you call it, stead of swillin' like a beast up to beerhouse.

JOAN: There, there, Dick, lad, don't 'ee go for to mad him. Speak un fair, lad—thy elder brother he be.

JOHN: (*mimicking*) Ah! speak un fair—You shut your head, Mother. I be good enough to stand up to Dick, I be. Who goes swillin' like a beast?

78

RICH: You do. They be fair shamed to speak to us, neighbours be. They be a drunken lot, them Perrys, they say—'Ah', they say, 'I see John Perry over to Aston. He were asleep in the ditch, the drunken sot!'

JOHN: Who say?

RICH: Parson say, and Farmer Hill say, and thy poor Mother say, and I say too, if they ben't good enough.

JOHN: Let un say! You be a lot of old puts, all on you—You leave I, I do advise thee. I won't take no preachin' from you. You be a old put, and Mother be.

RICH: Rather be a old put, than rotten fruit, you drunken dog, you!

JOHN: I ben't no drunken dog.

RICH: You be.

JOAN: Ah! Don't 'ee mad un now, Dick.

JOHN: Better be a drunken dog than a knuckler to Pa'son. You was always the good one, you was. You was like the good boy in the Bible, you always was. You was born to tread on my corns, you was, you closhy put.

RICH: I ben't no closhy put.

JOHN: You've crossed I long enough, Master Dick. You cross I no more, or I'll give you a cross 'll set thee i' the muck.

RICH: I don't cross thee, John, nor I never done.

JOHN: You be a liar! Wan't you a gettin' sixpence when I were a gettin' nought? Wan't it you got the hat give you? Wan't it you got Master's coat with the red trimmings? And I got nought. You with your pretty face, you grinning pinkanye! Wan't you a gettin' eight shillin' when I were a gettin' but seven? And I your elder, and your better.

DICK: You be my elder, but you ben't my better. If I got eight shillin' an' you seven, it's because I didn't

79

go swilling over to Aston. I didn't get drunk, I didn't.

JOHN: No, nor you hadn't got the soul in you, you mean. Then you comes a sucking and a trucking to Master Harrison—'Ah!' you says, 'ben't I a godly one? Ben't I proper and godly?' 'Ah!' you says— So you get took to be his servant. Wan't that a cross to me? Wan't I enough servant to him? I didn't want no knucklin' sniveller helping me. You call that not crossing, don't you? Ah!

JOAN: Now ha' done, John, ha' done. Don't 'ee mind thy brother Dick, John.

JOHN: But I will mind him, I tell 'ee. He have crossed me since we weren't that high. Ah! you dog, you. I be a drunken one, be I? You must get more than I get, must you? And my lady'll speak to you. 'Good mornin', Perry,' she'll say, 'Oh! what beautiful weather.' 'Good evenin', Dick,' she'll say, 'You ben't no sot, you ben't. You ben't like your brother John.'—No, no, you be a innocent lamb, you be; but you be warned! You have done of your crossing me— you dear sweet suckin' innocent lamb. You was him got sore knees from praying, you was, you dog of dogtown!

JOAN: Ah! John dear, do a done!

RICH: Now, don't you go calling names, John Perry. I'll tell you what you are. You're a disgrace; you'll come to a bad end. I never crossed you, and you know it. It's true I'm getting more than you. After Michaelmas I'll be getting more still. I'll be getting twelve shilling a week. If you'd do more, and drink less, you'd be getting the same.

JOHN: If I'd do more! Don't you preach to me. What's the good of doing more, with you stepping in over my head. Twelve shilling a week you're going to have, are you? You are not. You think yourself high in the world. You think you're a clever one. You think you'll do better than your brother. You will not. Not with me here. High in the world you think yourself with your twelve shilling. I'll bring you low—I'll bring you lower than the lowest.

RICH: It'll take a soberer man than you to do it.

JOHN: What'll it take?

JOAN: A dear! A dear! That ever I should see the day! Go home, Dick lad, you're only angering your brother.

JOHN: Lower than the lowest, I'll bring you. You shall drag in the dirt, you and your twelve shillin'!

RICH: I tell you it'll take a soberer man than you. Go home, man. Get someone to pump on you. You need sobering. I wonder you're not ashamed to talk that way afore your mother!

JOHN: Don't you learn me my duty, you Noll Crumwell's man, you Dicky Kill King!

RICH: What am I?

JOHN: A canting put. That's what you are—and a dog—A dirty twelve shilling sneck up of a Ledbury lawyer; but you mark me, I'll bring you down!

RICH: Go home and sleep it off, man. I'm sick of hearing you.

JOHN: What? What? Sick, are you? I'll make you sicker.

(*He flies at RICH: and grapples with him*)

JOAN: (*running to door*) Help! Help! Mrs Harrison!

(ENTER MRS HARRISON)

MRS H: Lord save us, and spare us! Good God, be good to us! Why, what's all this? Lord God's my mercy; why, Dick, why, John! John, what are you doing here? I thought I forbid you my kitchen. Dick, I'm ashamed of you! As for you, John, a gaol's the best place for you. Dick, I'm ashamed of you, fighting in your Master's kitchen, and with your own brother! You'd ought to be ashamed of yourself! It was enough to turn all the beer in the cellar, the noise you were making.

RICH: He began it, mum!

JOHN: You be a liar.

JOAN: Remember your duty.

MRS H: Now say a word more, John Perry, and I'll have you bound over. As for you, Dick, I'll tell your Master. Has your Master come in yet?

DICK: No 'm. Us haven't heard him.

MRS H: Lord God, be good to a sinful woman. If I haven't enough to bear! It's not enough that I have my house made a common bawdy house. Like a den of thieves it was, the noise you were making; and my man must go boozing till I don't know what hour.— It'll be another of his gallivaunts—I'll give him harvesting when he comes in. Go saddle the mare, one of you, and go to Charringworth and bring him back with you.

JOHN: (*Rising*) I'll go, give me the lantern, Mother.

DICK: You set down, John Perry. You ain't fit to bring any one home.

JOHN: Give I the lantern. (*To DICK*) I'll give you a bloody head if you orders me.

DICK: Set down, when you're told. Give me that light.

JOHN: No, you don't! Stand back. Would you? Take that! (*he hits him*)

JOAN: Ah, Lord! Ah, Lord! Don't 'ee, Dick, lad.

MRS H: Now, John, John Perry—Lord God's my hope and mercy. There'll be bloody adultery done. What, John, I say!

82

JOHN: I'll learn 'ee.

DICK: Let go of my throat, or I'll hit 'ee one.

JOAN: Ah dear! Ah dear! Oh, do 'ee.

MRS H: (*snatching a cider mug and dashing cider into JOHN'S face—the fighters separate*) Lord God's my hope and mercy! If I'm not all of a tremble—all of a tremble you've made me. And the cider all over my new taffety! Lord God's my witness, there might have been murder done. Get you out of this, John Perry. I do believe, John, as you'd do murder. Get you out of this. Never you darken these doors again. I believe as you'd cut my husband's throat— Lord Jesus have mercy—for what he had on him. Saddle the mare, Dick. You're the only one of the two I can trust. Saddle the mare, Dick. Where's my bottle of cordials?

(EXIT)

DICK: I knowed how it would be—and I get disgraced because you go swilling beer, and come here drunk. Give us the lantern. (*He lights it. John glowers at him*)

JOAN: Ah dear! ah dear! Ah, Dick, I do wish thee wouldn't mad thy brother. Ah dear! Ah dear! He be that like his poor feyther.

DICK: (*taking harness down*) You're a disgrace, you are. You're a disgrace to Campden— you're a disgrace to your mother. You make us shamed. Ugh, you drunkard!

(EXIT DICK WITH HARNESS AND LANTERN: *JOHN glowers after him*)

JOAN: (*in a quavering voice*) Ah dear, ah dear. I be getting old. It ben't like it were. There be none to comfort me now my man is taken. If thy poor feyther were alive now! Ah, John dear, don't 'ee mind thy brother Dick. Ah dear, he do mad thee, that he do. He do vex thee sore. Ah dear! I must

83

be getting home.—It be late. Don't 'ee mind thy brother Dick, John.

JOHN: I'll mind my brother Dick.

(*She goes out slowly after waiting a moment. JOHN glowers after her*)

JOHN: (*slowly*) Old Harrison be out late. They think he be gone away boozing, but he ben't. Only I know where old Harrison be gone. (*a pause*) Twelve shillin' a week you be gettin'. Twelve shillin' a week, and I nought but nine. (*The mare's hoofs sound outside*) Ah, ha, ha! I'll do it—That's what I'll do.

(RE-ENTER JOAN)

JOHN: I'll drag him lower than the low, him and his twelve shillin'.

JOAN: Do 'ee come, John. I be all of a shake.

JOHN: (*going*) Lower than the dirt, I'll drag him.

CURTAIN
(*The Curtain rises again immediately*)

SCENE II

SCENE: *The same.* MRS HARRISON AND THE PARSON. (DICK PERRY, *within*, *singing, and* JOAN *joining in the chorus, heard faintly*).

PARSON: Come, come, Mrs Harrison, bear a good heart! Come, don't take on so. Your husband's only—only gone to see a friend. He'll be back to dinner, I daresay.

MRS H: Not with the friends he goes to see, no. Oh, if I haven't much to bear.

PARSON: O, but, Mrs Harrison, come now, go in and take some breakfast. Why, your husband's well enough. Think, think of last year, what a turn

84

he gave us. No one would hurt Mr Harrison. It's absurd. Anyone would think he had been murdered.

MRS H: Murdered—ah! There's some comfort in a corpse. There's satisfaction in a body. I was saying that to Mrs Murrell. 'If one has the body,' I said, 'one knows one has done one's duty by it.' One knows that it's all for the best, and then there's the funeral. O dear, O dear—my man lying drunk in a ditch! It's his beer again—Beer, beer, beer. It's his ruin. O, if I had you here, William Harrison! O, a corpse would be a mercy compared to this. And half of my lady's corn not cut, and the reapers saying they must have another penny a day. O, William Harrison! Man is a trial, and a rod of affliction. It's a gnashing of teeth you've been to me.

(ENTER JOHN)

PARSON: Why, my good Mrs Harrison, this'll never do. Why, here's John Perry back. Come, John, you've brought good news, I'm sure. Come, Mrs Harrison, here's John back. Well, John, have you found Mr Harrison? Where was he?

JOHN: No, nor won't find him—Neither you nor no one.

PARSON: John!

JOHN: Neither you nor no one.

MRS H: There, now! If he hasn't been at the drink again. I smell it on him from here—like an empty cider cask. I think I've enough to bear without you getting drunk, John Perry.

JOHN: You have enough to bear—that's true.

PARSON: What do you mean, John, man? He's not drunk, Mrs Harrison. What is it? What has happened?

MRS H: You don't mean to say he was seen with Mrs Emsworth? I'm—

PARSON: Hush, Mrs Harrison—we are all in God's

hand. Speak John. Tell us! Speak, man, can't you?

JOHN: I want my words took down.

(*THE PARSON looks hard at him*)

MRS H: Is it as bad as that? He's been seen with the scarlet woman! He's been sitting on the seven hills. I know it. O dear, O dear, drinking the wine of wrath.

PARSON: Hush, Mrs Harrison. (*He sits down to ink and paper*) Now, John, tell us all you have to say. Mrs Harrison, we are but children, we must submit to Providence. We are here to declare the glory of God, not to cry over our little hurts. If Providence has taken your husband, you should rejoice. Now, John, speak, tell us everything. Come, Mrs Harrison.

(*The voices of DICK and JOAN within, singing*)

JOHN: I ben't going to tell my words, till there be witnesses. I want Tom Constable, and I want Mother here, and brother Dick. I got Tom Constable, outside. I brought 'en special.

PARSON: (*going to door*) Mrs Perry! Dick! Is Tom Constable, outside there still, or has he gone home?

DICK: (*within*) He be here, sir.

PARSON: Just ask him to step inside, and will you come in too, both of you?

(ENTER DICK, JOAN AND TOM CONSTABLE)

Stand at the door, Tom, and attend to what is said.

TOM: I will, sir.

PARSON: (*aside*) Mrs Perry, just get out the cordials, and set them by Mrs Harrison, I'm afraid she may swoon. (*she does so*) I want you all to attend to what John, there, has to say. Now, John, tell all you know.

JOHN: I ben't going to tell my words, not till I had my book-oath took.

PARSON: Lay your hand on this testament.

JOHN: (*putting hand on testament*) I be going to testify.

(a pause)

JOHN: I be going to testify. (*glowering at MRS. HARRISON*) Mrs Harrison, thee'd best drink a drop—I got awful news. I got awful news. Mr Harrison be dead.

PARSON: Be patient, Mrs Harrison, hear all. How dead?

JOHN: Murdered dead.

ALL: What?

JOHN: Murdered dead!

PARSON: (*standing up*) We are but children, Mrs Harrison. Whom God loveth he chasteneth. How was he murdered, John?

JOHN: I be going to testify. I want my words took down. (*PARSON takes pen*)—It was us murdered Mr Harrison.

ALL: What, what, what d'ye mean?

JOHN: It was I, and Mother, and Dick there, murdered Mr Harrison.

DICK: You—liar!

JOAN: Be you gone mad, John?

PARSON: Have a care what you say, John Perry.

JOHN: For his gold we murdered him.

MRS H: I don't believe a word you're saying— (*Weeps*)

JOHN: For his gold we murdered him.

DICK: I wonder God don't strike thee dead, John.

JOAN: John have gone crazed, sir. It be the sun —he were in the sun afore he took food this morning. Do 'ee sit, John. Us'll bathe thy poor head for 'ee.

JOHN: We murdered en dead for his gold. For his gold we murdered en,—didn't us, Dick?

87

DICK: Mr . . . Sir! God have afflicted my poor brother—He don't know what he say.

JOHN: I know what I say, I do. And you do. It lie black on my breast—It was your bloody mind planned it.

MRS H: You be a-lying, John Perry. You always was a liar! I was saying what a liar you was only yesterday, to Mrs Murrell I said it—'that John Perry be a liar,' I said. Where did you murder him? Where's the body?

JOHN: We murdered en dead for his gold.

DICK: Shall us put leeches to en's head, Sir? He be mazed. It be the blood. Shall I go fetch Doctor?

PARSON: (*in a hard voice*) Stay where you are, Richard Perry. Come here to the table—and you, Mrs Perry. Will you lay your hands to this testament and swear you are innocent of this crime? This crime John accuses you of?

DICK: Sir, you don't surely—sir, you don't go for to believe him? Sir, you don't go for to believe him?

JOAN: My poor boy be crazed, sir. Make 'en set, sir. He don't know what he do say.

PARSON: I ask you to put your hands to this testament, and swear you are innocent of this crime. This crime John here accuses you of.

DICK: Sir, you ben't thinking—O! God, sir, you ben't thinking that?

JOAN: I do swear it, Sir. I swear it purely. Do 'ee let me bathe his head now, Sir. It be only a wammering-like.

JOHN: It ben't no wammering. It lie black on my breast.

PARSON: Come here to the table, Dick Perry. I want you to swear—Put your hand on this testament.

DICK: (*aloud*) What be I to say, sir?

JOHN: Say how we killed en, Dick. Say how we laid en dead.

DICK: I say you be a wicked liar, John, a liar afore God. I say as I be false accused, and as Mother is. And I say you be a wicked liar, John, or you be smit mad.

JOHN: You come to me last night, you did. And Mother come—'Let's kill en', you said—And you'd said it afore. 'Let's kill en', you said—and Mother said it.

DICK: Parson, do believe en! (*a pause*)—God help my poor wife! (*he goes to testament*)—I do swear as I be false accused. As I be innocent—And as Mother be.

MRS H: And I believe thee, Dick. Thy brother John be a liar: to Mrs Murrell I said it. If he ben't swooning, now.

(*DICK puts his hand to his head, and sways a moment. He takes out a handkerchief, as he takes it out he drops some twine*)

JOHN: (*pouncing on the twine*) Now, what d'ye say, Dick Perry? 'Ee don't know this, do 'ee, now. What be this string, Dick? What be this, Mother?

DICK: It be my poor wife's hair net.

JOAN: Why, so it be. It be a hair net, to be sure.

PARSON: What do you know of this hair-string, John Perry? Do you know it?

JOHN: I know it, I do. And Mother know it, and Dick. To our cost we know it. It be the cord we murdered en with.

JOAN AND DICK: Oh, John Perry!

PARSON: Where was this? This that you say?

JOHN: Below Battle Ridge. At the foot o'hill it were. By the brook, where they found ens collar.

JOAN: Us was never nigh the place.

DICK: John, have done with thy sport. Say you

be fooling. Parson—Do 'ee think what 'ee be say-ing.

JOHN: I *do* think, I do. And *you* think. I con-fessed, I have. I made a clean breast—our sin be black—black it be—to kill poor Mr Harrison.

PARSON: Be calm, Mrs Harrison, hear all. (*he writes*) Now tell us how you killed him. Listen Tom, you will have to give evidence at the trial.

DICK AND JOAN: Sir, don't you believe en. Sir, you ben't goin' to believe en. He be lying, sir. Mrs Harrison knows he be lying. He be smit mad, sir.

PARSON: Keep silence, please. You will be heard in due course. Now, John.

JOHN: So brother Dick he says, 'Let's kill en'. 'For ens gold,' says Mother. Often they'd said it. So us goes out—

PARSON: What time was this?

JOHN: It were—it were twelve. So us goes out, and we see old Mr Harrison coming, singing. In the moonlight we seed en, and Dick and Mother and I, we strangles un—with this cord. O, it were a black deed!

MRS H: (*Interrupting*) John Perry, you be ly-ing—where's the body? I don't believe as my poor man be dead. Nor I won't. Not till I touch his cold corpse—there now.

PARSON: Where is the body, John?

JOHN: Mother and Dick took ens body. They were hardened uns, they were. I were that shook by our black deed! O, a black deed it were. Where did 'ee put ens corpse, Mother? Hey, Dick?

DICK: (*To PARSON*) Sir, he be play-acting. You see he be play-acting.

JOAN: If my poor man were alive, us wouldn't be like this, us wouldn't. Do 'ee not damn thy soul black, John. Thou knows us be innocent.

JOHN: A proper hardened un, you was; and Dick was.

PARSON: Richard Perry, can you now, in the sight of God, put your hand on this testament, and swear yourself innocent, after what John here has said? Can you, Mrs Perry?

MRS P: I be a poor old widow woman, I be. I an't got no man, I an't, not since my poor man were took. Seventy year have I lived in Campden, and some time it have been hard, and some time it have been not so hard; and us have had our little home, us have, though us were poor. I have brought my sons up in the fear of the Lord. I wasn't never questioned like this afore. Us have borne a good name, us have, though us were poor. I be innocent, Sir. God forgive my poor lying boy.

JOHN: God forgive thee leading I to murder.

PARSON: Now, Richard Perry.

MRS H: Dick be fainting. (*to PARSON*) It be a cruel shame, it be, sir, to vex us so. For shame, Sir.

DICK: I be innocent, I be. John knows I be innocent. My poor wife knows I be, and Mother knows. (*He touches book and sways*)

PARSON: His nose is bleeding. It is the hand of God. God hath spoken, Tom.

TOM: Ess, sir.

PARSON: Call thy men.

(*TOM goes to door and whistles*)

DICK: What be 'ee going to do, please, sir. Us have sworn.

(ENTER MEN)

PARSON: Tom Constable, take John here, and Dick, and Mrs Perry, to the lock-up.

DICK: Sir, do 'ee now!

TOM: Thee'd best come quiet, Dick. Us won't hurt 'ee.

91

DICK: But I be innocent. It be a lie. I ben't no murderer.

PARSON: You will be able to prove that at your trial. Remove them, Tom.

JOHN: Our blood be due for our black deed—Us shall all hang.

JOAN: Give me thy arm, Tom. I be a old woman. I ain't got no man, I an't. Book says us must be patient. (*she goes to JOHN and strokes his face*) John, boy, thee be that like thy dad, John. Us must get Doctor to un, mustn't us, Dick? (*she makes her reverence to PARSON*)

TOM: Come, mother, lean on my arm.

DICK: Bear on me, Mother. (*They support her to door*)

JOAN: (*turning at door*) Mrs Harrison, us be poor folk, false accused. Do 'ee get Doctor to look to my poor boy.

JOHN: Us shall be like Staffordshire—three hung in one knot.

PARSON: Do your office, Tom.

(EXEUNT CONSTABLES &C.
MANENT PARSON & MRS HARRISON)

Bear up, Mrs Harrison. We are like the old lanterns in the hall—we are dark—we are broken. And anon God takes us, and sets us on the walls of Heaven, amid unspeakable beauty, to light His Courts. Your husband—

MRS H: Mr Parson, sir. You be a man of God, and you be a scholard. It don't beseem the likes of me to talk plain to the likes of you. You'd ought to go down on your knees and ask forgiveness. You be swift to shed innocent blood. *You* talk of lanterns, and such. Down on your knees, you ought to go. You've been and committed them Perrys on the word of a liar and a dog. My man ben't murdered—my man ben't murdered. That John Perry'd hang his mother for a sup of drink.

PARSON: Mrs Harrison, John Perry would not accuse himself; you forget yourself.

MRS H: Forget myself, do I! In my own house—quotha! Ladida indeed—so I forget myself! You be a sneck up of a covetuous Levite, a creeping into widows' houses. That's what you be. Ladida indeed! But I ben't no widow. When my man comes home he shall reckon with thee, he shall. And the Perrys shall. They'll teach 'ee to shed innocent blood on the word of a dog and a liar. Marry, come up!

(EXIT PARSON)

O, Willy Harrison, Willy Harrison! You and your beer will be my death!

C U R T A I N

S C E N E III

(*A room in the lock-up at Broad Campden.* MRS PERRY, DICK, JOHN, *secured by wrists and ankles to chains. They are in different corners. A table in front*)

JOAN: Us be to die, Dick. Do 'ee bear up, lad. Thou, knows John, as us be innocent. And God he knows it. Us shall have mercy, Dick. Us shall walk the gold streets and that—for ever, Amen.

DICK: It be easy for you to talk, Mother. I do think of my poor wife, I do, and of my poor babes. 'There goes his wife,' they'll say. That's what neighbours'll say. 'Him as killed poor Mr Harrison.'

JOHN: 'As killed him for uns gold.'

DICK: John, do 'ee now speak. Say as us be innocent. Don't ee see us hanged, boy. There be my

93

poor wife, and my poor babes. Do ee speak, John, speak. Her'll be but a tramp, and my little Nan and all. Her were saying so pretty—And I shan't see un again. Lord, never again! And her'll want bread to eat, and go to bed crying. Do ee speak, John. For God's sake, John, say as us be innocent.

JOHN: Us'll have ballads sung—and I shouldn't wonder. Us'll all be in a ballad. 'The bloody Perrys, they was hanged—O, grief!' And there'll be drums, and the sun a-shining—on Broadway Hill and all. And there'll be neighbours. Sure to be. And us'll go in a cart, like high up folk. 'There they go'; neighbours'll say, 'as killed un for ens gold. They was always bad ones, them Perrys,' they'll say.

JOAN: John, thou be going afore thy Maker, thou be. Us be going to die to-day. It be a sad thing for a old woman to die with her sons—her two boys, as she's been that proud of. To be hanged up on a hill with neighbours calling her a old witch. And then, there be Dick's little maids. O, John, do 'ee speak, lad! And us won't be put in churchyard. I shan't lie with my poor man, a dear! Whatever will I do, a dear! I shan't lie with my poor man!

JOHN: I ben't going to speak, I ben't. I said my say. To Judge I said it. Her were all in her red gownd. 'Ah, you Perry,' he said: 'you be a notable rogue.' Her had a sword afore her. Now us be going to be hanged. I wonder will us have ale give us. Old Cop of Aston, they give *him* ale.

(ENTER TOM CONSTABLE)

TOM: Master Parson, sir.

JOAN: He ben't here—yet—Tom.

TOM: Can I do aught for ee, Mrs Perry?

JOAN: Us be past it, Tom, I do thank ee. It be my boy, John, and my boy, Dick, as I be grieved for. And them little maids of Dick's. Us be false accused, us be, my poor mad boy knows. And God knows. And them little ones'll want bread when us be gone!

TOM: Mrs Harrison have took Dick's little ones. God save ee, Mother. Us knows as you be innocent. And neighbours says it. God bless ee, Dick, if I don't see ee again.

DICK: God bless ee for thy kind words. Ee comfort poor Nan, Tom. Don't ee let folk say as her Daddy were hung. God comfort my poor Nan.

TOM: God bless ee, Dick, lad, and comfort ee. God forgive ee, John. Thy hands be red of blood, John; God forgive ee. (*To PARSON*) Saving your presence, sir.

PARSON: Go, Tom.

(EXIT TOM)

JOAN: I be ready, sir. I be ready to go in the cart.

PARSON: Ah, Mrs Perry! In a few moments you will be before God's Judgment Seat, a trembling bird on God's hand. How will you ask mercy of Him, when you have hardened your heart here on earth; denying the guilt for which you suffer!

JOAN: I ben't afeard to meet my God, sir. God have pity upon the poor and on the widows. I be innocent of blood, I be. I've been a great sinner, and I be punished for it. I set my boy John afore my boy Dick. Parson, I be dying. Will ee let I lie in Chrisom ground? Let I lie near my man, Parson, along of my poor husband?

(ENTER TOM)

TOM: (*in a choking voice*) It be the Sheriff, sir.

PARSON: Come, Mrs Perry. You are about to walk in Paradise, among the holy ones. You are about to stand before God, in the glory unspeakable. Lean on me—lean on Tom here.

95

JOAN: John, won't ee say now as we be false accused? Ee won't see thy old mother hanged? Do ee speak. Say as you spoke lies, John. Thee knows ee did.

DICK: For God's sake, John.

JOHN: I confessed to Parson, and I confessed to Judge, I ben't bound to confess to you.

JOAN: God have mercy on us all then. May He have mercy on you, John—And on you, Dick—and on me, thy mother—and on all poor souls. May us meet glorified in God's golden courts, Amen.

PARSON: Amen. Come, Mrs Perry.

JOAN: God be with ee, Dick. I've put ee to bed, Dick, a many times. But now I be going to bed afore you.

DICK: God be with ee, Mother. God comfort ee.

JOAN: God be with ee, too, John. For all your sins.

(She turns to go)

Ee be that like thy poor feyther, John. I be going to God's holy house.

TOM: Lean on me, Mother.

(They go out at door—the drums beat up)

JOHN: O, us be going to have drums.

DICK: Thou be a dog, John, thou be. O, John, say as us be innocent, say it out, now. It'll save Mother. It'll save my little Nan. . . Call, John; call! O, John, thou be a dog!

JOHN: Call, Dick. That be right. Call, Dick. Shout! Thy throat it won't call much longer.

DICK: Ah, God!

JOHN: O! It be 'Ah, God' now, be it! It were 'I be a proper godly one,' it's not so long since. How about thy twelve shillin' a week, Dick? You that was to be that high in the world? Eh, Dick? Thy twelve shillin'? Lower than the dirt I've dragged ee.

Like I said I'd do. Lower than the dirt, thou and thy twelve shillin'.

DICK: Then thee ben't mad. Thee've sworn our lives away!

JOHN: You be a clever one, you be!

(RE-ENTER PARSON, *very white and sick, and* TOM)

DICK: Parson, John have confessed. He've confessed he have sworn false. O! Parson, do ee save Mother. He have confessed, sir.

JOHN: He be mazed, sir. Give un a cordial, Parson. He be clean mazed.

DICK: O, Sir, hear en. Do ee save Mother. Her said he'd done it a purpose to cross I. Do ee listen, sir.

PARSON: Come, Richard Perry. Compose yourself. We are poor flames blowing in the wind, now one way, now another. In the peace of God's house our light will burn steadily. Come, Richard Perry.

(TOM *undoes chains*)

DICK: God help my poor wife. God help all dying men as folk won't listen to! I've lived honest, and I've worked honest, and this be the end.

PARSON: It is but the beginning. There is no end to the glory and the peace of God.

DICK: (*To JOHN*) And no end to the fire for such as thee, John. May the red hot worms gnaw thy body, John. You dog, you dog!

PARSON: Come, Dick. Help him, Tom.

DICK: O Parson, do ee make John speak. He have confessed, sir. O! sir, he have confessed. Indeed, sir, he've confessed. Make un speak, Parson. It'll save my Nan.

PARSON: Come, Dick. It is but a step. Do not seek to stay longer in this wicked world.

DICK: But he've confessed, Parson. He've said as he were lying. O! sir, do ee.

JOHN: Give un a cordial, Parson. He be fair mazed. Help en, Tom.

TOM: Come, be a man, Dick!

(EXEUNT—*The drums again*)

JOHN: There he do go, him and his twelve shillin'. Ah, you godly one! Ha, you godly one! They got you. Lower than the dirt, like as I said I'd do. Afore all Campden! You and your twelve shillin'! Make un a speech, Dick. Make thy speech and confession. O! if I might see thee. O! if only door were open. Thee be looking pale, you and your twelve shillin'. You that thought to be high in the world. Aha! Aha!

(*A cry without and drums*)

There he do go! Aha! Aha!

(*A pause*)

(RE-ENTER PARSON AND TOM)

PARSON: O! the pity of it, the pity of it! O! Lord strengthen me.

JOHN: Mr Parson, Sir, might I speak to ee, sir?

PARSON: In a minute. In a minute, John. O! Lord, have pity.

JOHN: I be a dying man, Parson. I got summat to say to ee.

(PARSON STANDS)

Parson, will ee give I comfort? I been a great sinner, I have. I been drunk, and I stole; and I been poaching, and I gone with women. And I kill poor Mr Harrison. O! I been a black one, I have. Shall I have mercy, Parson? Be I doomed to the fire?

PARSON: There is joy, John, over one sinner that repenteth. God's mercy is infinite. Put your trust in Him, John.

JOHN: Ah, sir. I do feel it in my heart. It be a glow, like.

98

PARSON: Come, John Perry.

(TOM UNDOES CHAINS)

There is yet one thing, John. Where is Mr Harrison's body? You are about to die, John. Tell us this, that he may have Christian burial.

JOHN: It were Dick and Mother took his body, sir. I don't know where it be, I don't. But perhaps one day you'll find en. You'll be wiser on that day, Parson.

PARSON: You talk strangely, John.

JOHN: A dying man have a right to talk strange. I be ready, Sir. Will you say a prayer for me, Sir? "Our Father" or summat.

PARSON: Repeat it after me, John. Come.

(EXEUNT: DRUMS AGAIN)

(*A pause, during which the drums beat. Then a march as the troops pass away*)

(ENTER MRS HARRISON, PANTING)

MRS H: Are you there, Dick? Ah! Ah! If I'm not near my death. Are you there, Dick? Mrs Perry!

(ENTER PARSON. *MRS H. fans herself. PARSON mops his brow*)

PARSON: The wages of sin is death. (*He mops and sits down*) The wages of sin is death. He talked strangely. And the old woman—Ah, God, her gray hairs—and then the frantic one, about his child. Ah, have pity, O Father! The wages of sin is death, death. It has been a terrible day. A terrible day.

MRS H: What's terrible? How has it been terrible? What ails you, man?

PARSON: (*looking at her*) O, Mrs Harrison—

MRS H: Oh? Well, he's come home, like I said he would.

PARSON: Who?

99

MRS H: Who? Why, William Harrison, my husband.

PARSON: Come home?

MRS H: Yes, come home, like I said he would.

PARSON: Come home?

MRS H: If you don't vex a sinful woman's flesh! Yes, he has come home—boozing—That's where he's been.

(PARSON COVERS HIS EYES AND MOANS)

(*aloud*) Now, don't set there moaning—You've got to set them Perrys free.

(SHE GOES TO HIM AND SHAKES HIM)

Go and find 'em, and set 'em free. Come, come, now, don't ee take it to heart. We all make mistakes. That John Perry, he might have had 'em all hanged.

PARSON: (*weakly*) They are—all hanged.

MRS H: What?

PARSON: Hanged. This morning.

MRS H: But it was to-morrow.

PARSON: No, to-day.

MRS H: But this be the sixteenth? This be Tuesday?

PARSON: No. (*a long pause*)

MRS H: So that's why the town was empty. That's why the prison's got no—(*fiercely*) Be you telling the truth?

PARSON: O, don't, don't!

(*a pause*)

MRS H: May God be good to a sinful woman.

PARSON: Amen.

MRS H: They be happy to be out of such a world.

PARSON: "O, Father, Now is my soul troubled, and what shall I say?"

MRS H: Us be two poor souls, Parson.

(CRYING AND LAYING HER HAND ON HIS)

C U R T A I N

MRS. HARRISON

MRS. HARRISON

PERSONS

WILL HARRISON

PARSON

TOM CONSTABLE

MRS. HARRISON

MRS. HARRISON

SCENE: *A Room in MRS HARRISON'S House*

MRS H. There's your cider. Take it; there's a toast in it. Take it. And now, you and I will have a reckoning.

WILL H. Huh!

MRS H. (*Rapping table*) You may groan and you may grunt, but you'll listen to me. And you'll answer me. You'll answer me, before you leave this room.

WILL H. Gerr yer.

MRS H. I want to know about you, William Harrison. A nice husband you've been to me. And now I want to know about you, and you'll answer me. Wher've you been all this long while? Wher've you been, I say? What Dolly Draggletails have you been with?

WILL H. Ah, put your head in a bag!

MRS H. Put my head in a bag! Put my head in a bag! You low dog, you. There's a way to talk to a woman. There's a way to talk to a wife. How dare you tell me put my head in a bag. How dare you, after what's past? How dare you? After leaving me alone all this long while. Is this a world to leave a woman alone in? Is this a world to leave a nice, comely, decent, fine-grown woman alone in? Let alone your wife!

WILL H. Huh! I run no risks leaving you.

105

MRS H. No. So you ran no risks, didn't you? There's some would have said different. There's some set a higher price on beauty than what you do. A comely woman's something to them, it is.

WILL H. It is, is it? They're welcome!

MRS H. When you've done with your insults, we'll talk. Where've you been all this long while?—You've been with your beer and your dollymops!——I'm sick to think I've kissed you.

WILL H. And I am.

MRS H. Thank you. Thank you for nothing. And now I want an answer. When you've done with your sneers and your jeers I want an answer. D'ye know what you've done by going away? D'ye know what your beer and your trollopsing have been the cause of?

WILL H. I know what your naggin's 'll be the cause of. Here—(*he bangs mug*)—Cider.

MRS H. You'll answer me first.

WILL H. Cider, I say.

MRS H. You have been the cause of three folk being hanged;—John Perry, and Dick Perry and poor old Mrs Perry;—Hanged. Hanged by the neck! That's a fine thing, isn't it, for beer and trulls to do? Wher've you been, you tank, you dog, you low thing. Where've you been? What can you say for yourself?

WILL H. Gimme my cider. Gimme my cider when I tell you!

MRS H. (*Snatching cider mug.*) Here! (*She smashes it on floor and stamps on fragments*) There! That's all the cider you'll get. Now, answer.

WILL H. (*Getting up and snatching her wrist*) Be that the game? Well, I'll answer. Sit down there. And you say another word, and you'll get a knock'll give you sense! I'll tell you where I've been; and keep it dark. You'd better. You speak a word of it, and you'll be missed. The first dark night as comes, you'll be missed.

MRS H. That means you'll murder me.

WILL H. Listen! I went away acos I was paid to go away. D'ye understand that? Paid.

MRS H. Who paid you?

WILL H. Ah! Wouldn't you? And I was paid three hundred golden pound to go away. And my going away was worth that to the man as paid it.

MRS H. Where did ee go to?

WILL H. I weren't never more'n twenty mile away.

MRS H. Then ee knew. Ee knew of what—ee knew of the Perrys?

WILL H. I knowed all about the Perrys.

MRS H. You knowed about the Perrys?

WILL H. And glad to.

MRS H. You knowed they was to be hanged?

WILL H. And glad to.

MRS H. And 'ee could have saved 'en.

WILL H. I knowed one worth two of that. You listen to I and keep your mouth shut. John Perry knew where I were. And why I'd gone. Think I'd let 'en live when he were that crazy to go and get hanged? Think I'd stop 'en hanging when he knew my secret? Gerr yer; talk sense!

MRS H. Then you let them poor souls be hanged, knowing they was innocent.

WILL H. Ah, talk sense.

MRS H. You set by and let them all be hanged?

WILL H. Didn't I tell you I got three hundred pound? What's the Perrys to me? I know my duty, I hope. Hark you to me, missus. It was my Lord give me that £300. It was to my Lord's advantage I should be away awhile. What's three Perrys, or six Perrys, or a churchful of Perrys to my Lord?

Hark you to me! (*he gets up and goes to her*) And you breathe so much as a shuddering, wee glimmer of a whisper,—you just raise your little dove-like voice— you just dare to! (*he snaps his fingers*) And it'll be your last.

MRS H. (*slowly*) And—I'm—to—live—with— a —murderer? I've had a murderer to bed with me, and held 'en in my arms! (*to WILL H.*) And what tale will you tell the neighbours? What tale am I to tell the neighbours when they ask? Lord God! if it ben't pitiful!

WILL H. Damn the neighbours! Gimme my cider.

MRS H. There's footsteps coming up the walk. It'll be parson. O God, Will, what be I to tell en?

(A KNOCK AT THE DOOR)

WILL H. Why, tell 'en—tell 'en—Tell 'en something; you'd better. Say I was kidnapped. And bear me out, now. Bear me out in that. I was kidnapped. (*Another knock*) Set down there, (*she sits*) and now, remember. You say a word of the truth, (*he snaps his fingers*)—your neck'll go like that!—Come in! Who be there?

(ENTER TOM CONSTABLE AND PARSON)

Why, if it bain't you, parson. Come in. Come in! Why now, if this ben't strange. What wonders I have to tell 'ee.

PARSON O Harrison. There have been wonders indeed. To think of you coming home safely, after all. Your wife is looking quite white, even now. I don't wonder.

WILL H. They do say as joy kills quicker'n grief, parson.

PARSON You must look after Mrs Harrison. It has been a terrible time for her.

TOM Ah! it has.

WILL H. (*recognising TOM*) Why, Tom. Tom Constable. And how be you, Tom? Why, what joy it be to meet all the old folk agen.

TOM Thank 'ee, sir. I be doing kindly, sir.

PARSON Yes, I brought Tom as a witness. I have to write to my Lord and tell him everything. Ah me, it is a terrible tale! And so you've come back?

WILL H. They do say as seein' is believin'.

PARSON Just to think, Mrs Harrison. Ah, Mrs Harrison! And so you've come back. O! if you had but come a day sooner. No, not a day; an hour; twenty minutes.

WILL H. We be in God's hands, parson.

PARSON It is the truth. And where've you been? Tell me now. Tell me everything. *Everything*!

WILL H. Well, you'll think there's still miracles.

MRS H. He was kidnapped, parson; think of that, kidnapped.

WILL H. By a man on horseback.

MRS H. By two men on horseback.

PARSON Where was this? Was this where they found the collar?

MRS H. Yes, by Battle Ridge. They wore masks; and they seized him.

TOM Why didn't 'ee welt their nags? I'd a welted en, afore they'd seized I.

MRS H. How could an old man fight agenst two?

PARSON Yes,——and then?

WILL H. Why then..... Why.... Let me see. Yes. So they said.... No a said nothing... They up and.... How were it now? (*Aside to MRS. H*) Help me out or I'll hit 'ee one.

MRS H. They up and set you afore one of them. You told me just now.

109

WILL H. Ah, they did. Afore one of them they set me.

MRS H. And he'd been eating onions, parson. Think of that. The one he set afore had been eating onions. Think of him noticing that. Think of a man noticing that.

PARSON Go on, go on.

WILL H. So they set me afore one of them. And he'd been eating onions. I could never abide the smell. No. I never could abide onions. Did you ever know me abide the smell of onions?

MRS H. No, you never did. You never could abide onions.

WILL H. They do say as one man's meat be another's poison—

PARSON So then?

WILL H. Why, all in good time..... So then..... Where was I? So then... You be in such a hurry... Why.... So then... I wish 'ee'd not interrupt.

MRS H. Here, William Harrison. If you aren't a trial and a torment. Do for goodness' sake let me tell the story!

TOM Ah, do 'ee.

PARSON Go on, Mrs Harrison.

MRS H. So they rode him off, oh, for miles. And then they came to a house, and they locked him in a room for all the next day. And at night they rode him off agen. And so on for a day or two. And then they came to a ship. And there he heard 'em selling his body for a slave. Selling his body for a slave—a slave to the Turk!

PARSON How much did they give for you, William?

WILL H. I heard one of them say thirty shillin'.

PARSON But that couldn't have been for you. That'd never have paid taking you across England.

MRS H. It'd be more like thirty pound.

110

WILL H. Well, it might a been pound. Thirty pound then.

MRS H. And then the ship was at sea, and at last they come to the Turks' country, where they sold him for a slave.

PARSON To think of that now! A Campden man a slave to the Turk!

TOM O Lord! thy wonders!

WILL H. I was a slave to the Turk.

PARSON What work did you do, William?

WILL H. Why hard work. Hard work it was.

MRS H. He was a slave to a doctor, parson,—digging in the herb beds.

WILL H. I dug 'em with a spade.

TOM I'd a liked to a seen 'ee dig, master.

PARSON And how did you get away, William?

WILL H. Well, I got away, didn't I,—though I be old.

TOM Old and bold as the saying is.

PARSON Ah, but how?

MRS H. His master sent him to an English merchant with a bottle of elixir. The merchant was sick. And William said he was an Englishman as had been stole away. And the merchant put 'en in a ship. And so he came home.

PARSON What port did you land at?

WILL H. (*puzzled*) It was Norfolk, I do think.

MRS H. Norfolk my grandmother! *Portsmouth* don't I keep telling you. (*to PARSON*) I think my man would make a saint cross. *Portsmouth*, Will. Norfolk's in France.

WILL H. Ah, *Portsmouth*. I be'n't no learned astronomer. One place be like another to me. I don't hold with these new fangled towns. I been a slave to the Turk. Give I Campden.

TOM O, the wonders of the Lord!

111

PARSON Well, Will; you ought to write a book.

WILL H. I don't know about any book. The Christian religion's book enough. There's a book. All else is sin, books is.

TOM Ah!

PARSON Now, Will. I want you to come up to the church with me to return thanks for your restoration, and to ask His mercy for our sins, and for the deaths of his innocents, the Perrys.

WILL H. Ah, that I will, Parson.

(They turn to go)

PARSON Come, Mrs Harrison.

MRS H. I be feeling overcome, Parson, I'll stay here and read the Bible, while you prays.

PARSON You must take care of yourself, Mrs Harrison. You must look after your wife, William. She has had a grievous trial.

WILL H. She'll pull round, you'll find. Joy cometh in the morning.

MRS H. Have I been a good wife to you, Will?

PARSON She's been overwrought, William.

MRS H. Have I been a good wife to you, Will?

WILL H. Now don't 'ee fuss. Set quiet. She'll be all right; she just needs letting alone a while. Come, parson, us'll just step to church.

(EXIT PARSON AND WILL H. *TOM holds door for them*)

MRS H. *(as TOM goes)* Tom!

TOM Yes, Mrs Harrison?

MRS H. Come here, Tom.

(TOM goes to table)

MRS H. Reach me the Bible.

TOM Here it be, miss.

MRS. H. Now, Tom.

TOM Yes, Mrs Harrison.

MRS. H. You know them little girls of Dick Perry's?

112

TOM   Ay!

MRS H.   You'll look after them little girls, Tom?

TOM   I said I'd do.   And I will do.

MRS H.   You'll not let folk say as their daddy were hung?

TOM   I'll break their heads as says it.   They'll not say it twice, if they says it once.

MRS H.   You'll swear that, Tom, swear it on the Bible.

TOM   There be'n't no call to swear, mum.   You knows me, I hope.

MRS H.   Swear it.   Swear you'll look after 'em. . Whatever happens. . .

TOM   What I can do I'll do.

MRS H.   (*going to a drawer*)   This be for you, Tom, to spend for them little girls.   It be what I got by my hens.   It be near five pound in silver.

TOM   I don't ask no money, I be glad to do a kindness.   I don't ask no money.

MRS H.   Take it.   Take it, I say!   And may the Lord prosper you for all you do for them poor little maids.   Look after 'em, Tom.

TOM   I'll look after 'em, mum.

MRS H.   Now go, Tom.   I be all-to frushed and of a frammock.

TOM   Can I get 'ee anything?

MRS H.   No, Tom.   Now 'ee go.

TOM   Good day to 'ee, mum.

MRS H.   God save 'ee, Tom.

(EXIT TOM)

MRS H.   I been wife to a murderer. . .   I been wife to a murderer. . .   I've been to bed with a man as done murder; and I've helped un clear after. . . .   (*she rocks in her chair; then gets up and goes to cupboard*)   But never no more, William Harrison, you've had your last of me. . . .   (*she opens cupboard*)   I be the lowest of the low. O Lord, I be the lowest of the low. . . . I feel as I'd been spat on. (*she rummages among bottles*) But never no more, William Harrison. . . . God have mercy on a sinful woman. . . . You've had your last of me, William Harrison. You can go to your Jennies, you can. . . . (*she takes out a paper*) This is it. This is it,—is the cure. I bought it for the rattens as ate my chicks. What'll kill rattens'll kill folk. Where be my thimble? (*she pours powder into thimble and drinks*) Ugh! it be bitter! (*she pours again and drinks*) Ugh! (*she puts thimble and paper into fire. The fire spurts up*) Ah, pretty it be! (*she goes to table and begins to read the Bible: she spells it out slowly*)

"But when Jesus saw it, he was much displeased, and said unto them: Suffer the little children to come unto me. Suffer the little children to come unto me." Us be little children—"And forbid them not.". . . It be a long road for poor folk. . . It be a cold road for us, poor children. . . . (*dies*)

THE END